JOHN HUGHES

BRIGHT BEWILDERING GREEN

WITH A FOREWORD BY JOHN STALKER

THE LILLIPUT PRESS
1991

First published in 1991 by
THE LILLIPUT PRESS LTD
4 Rosemount Terrace, Arbour Hill,
Dublin 7, Ireland

Acknowledgements
To my friend, John Stalker; to my editor,
Jilly Siddall; to my typist, Maureen Bateman;
and to Oliver Fagan for a pint and his untiring faith.

A CIP record for this
title is available from
The British Library

ISBN 0 946640 73 4

Set in | Galliard by
Koinonia of Manchester
and printed in Dublin by
Colour Books of Baldoyle

To Susy Hughes
whose gentle bullying awoke my inner self

I saw the sunlit vale, and the pastoral fairy-tale;
The sweet and bitter scent of the may drifted by;
And never have I seen such a bright bewildering green,
But it looked like a lie,
Like a kindly meant lie.

When gods are in dispute, one a Sidney, one a brute,
It would seem that human sense might not know, might not
spy;
But though nature smile and feign where foul play has stabbed
and slain,
There's a witness, an eye,
Nor will charms blind that eye.

(Edmund Blunden, 'The Sunlit Vale')

Foreword

❧

I first met John Hughes a dozen or so years ago on a bitterly cold February night. I watched him drive, for no discernible reason, twice round a Coventry roundabout followed too closely by a pair of suspicious policemen whose car skidded on the ice and crashed into his. During the next few minutes I witnessed the art of the gifted salesman as John Hughes persuaded the policemen they were entirely in the wrong but out of respect for them he would take the matter no further. I hold precious the memory of two apologetic policemen loading bits of their patrol car into the back seat and clattering away into the night. It was then I decided John Hughes was an interesting man.

Out of that meeting has grown a friendship based, I suppose, on the attraction of opposites. When it began I was a senior detective officer in a high profile public job, he a retail businessman worrying about interest rates and cash flow. We disagreed about many things; for example his political thoughts are not always mine and his total (and declared) disinterest in my sporting loves of athletics and Manchester United are usually matched by my numb response towards his preferred pastimes of weight-lifting and competitive clay-pigeon shooting. Yet our differences have been the catalyst for our friendship: the antidote to the stresses of our respective jobs. In recent years life for both of us has moved dramatically on: I am no longer a policeman and John Hughes's restless spirit has turned its energies in other business directions. Much has changed.

But, despite the closeness of our enduring friendship, I have always known I did not really know him. Not that he is a secretive man; indeed with people he likes and trusts he is often vulnerably open, but he was unfailingly uncomfortable with discussions about childhood influences or why people turn out the way they do. Over-curiosity about his early life was deflected by a directness close to rudeness. The John Hughes I have known since 1978 has been a man of here and now and like the rest of his friends I learned to understand that whatever the past contained it belonged to a different John Hughes, the shadow of whom we were unlikely ever to see.

But in this book that shadow becomes substance and at the end of it the child he was holds the hand of the man he became. Like many before him, John Hughes has found that a peaceful mind demands that the demons of the past be faced, and one way of doing it is to fight them with a pen in your hand. He confided in me a year or so ago that he had begun writing and I promised him that I would write a foreword if his efforts were considered good enough for commercial publication.

Bright Bewildering Green is the result. A story remarkable not because it is unusual but because it was – and still is – commonplace in rural Ireland: the story of the surplus child, the tragedy of the extra mouth. He has written a first-hand account of family resentment and cruelty, and of countervailing affection and hope leading him to a successful new life.

The book will surprise many people who know the author. I confess that the quality of the writing surprises me, from a man who cheerfully admits to having read only a couple of books in his life. But when did human talent not have the element of surprise? And since when was the writing of a readable book the preserve of educated men?

Bright Bewildering Green is a simple story told by the man to whom it happened. I am glad to have read it.

John Stalker

Manchester, January 1991

Preface

W̶hen I began to write this book I worried constantly about the pain and embarrassment it might cause my family. Gradually my anxieties receded as several powerful reasons to continue took command. First, I had to exorcize the ghost of my childhood which had haunted me for over twenty years. Secondly, I believed the story should be told, if only to try and reach those who suffer as I did. Finally, if I did not tell the story no one else would, and a chance for the voice of an ordinary man to be heard would have been lost yet again. Death strikes early in my family: mother died at forty-five and both father and William, my eldest brother, at forty-eight. So I decided to crack on.

I was unaware of the obliteration that had taken place until I tried to remember basic details of my family history. With the patient help of a London genealogist and my cousin Joseph Hughes, I eventually pieced together a picture of my fragmented background.

In 1984 I sought help from a hypnotherapist because although I had become skilled at clay-pigeon shooting, the winning of championships repeatedly eluded me, often prompting nervous attacks that shattered my confidence.

After weeks of counselling, the therapist asked if I was prepared to talk about my childhood. Reluctantly I agreed when he said that the root of the problem lay in my early life and that he could only help if I talked it through with him. I told him about the violence, my diagnosis of epilepsy at the age of fourteen and the years on medication. He asked

1

me how long I had taken Mysoline tablets for and when I replied that I had given them up after five years although the medical reports had recommended seven, his obvious relief concerned me. He explained that Mysoline was still one of Britain's major tranquillizers which could have horrendous long-term effects and that I was lucky to still be in possession of my senses and not reduced to a mindless wanderer. He seemed intrigued by what he called my amazing constitution until I reminded him of why I was there. He told me that my problem was easily diagnosed, that I had a victory phobia. Because I had been told as a youngster that I was hopeless, in moments of extreme pressure I still believed it.

I followed his course of relaxation therapy and in 1985 represented England in the Home Counties International Sporting Clay Pigeon Championship, hosted in Ireland. Being an Irishman going home to shoot for England gave me a strange feeling of revenge that I did not enjoy.

I gave no more thought to my supposed childhood illness until the writing of this book when, in a quest for the truth, I confronted my own doctor. He read out a letter from the doctors in Ireland written twenty-five years earlier, which stated: 'The results of the EEG are mildly unstable for age. This is not symptomatic with epilepsy but we have decided to treat it as such and suggest that you continue to do so.'

My doctor, who had recently taken over the practice, felt that it was unlikely I was ever an epileptic and added that nowadays the treatment I received would be highly controversial. When I asked him to read out another letter from my file he was perplexed and asked how I knew such a letter existed. I confessed that ten years earlier I had been left alone in the surgery for a moment and stole a look at my file. My furtive reading was short-lived, but I had managed to glean the opening sentence.

'This poor wee lad who has suffered much trauma and violence …'

The letter was missing. I left the surgery disappointed

that I could not pursue the matter and my suspicion that something was wrong grew deeper.

When I discovered that a law passed in 1988 gave me the right to inspect my records my doctor was most helpful and reopened the files. All that existed of the EEG report was a three-line extract stating:

'There were no epileptic waves found, or focus seen.'

None of the correspondence bore a signature, nor the name of the hospital or consultant concerned. Though my doctor assumed that the reports had been reduced to make filing easier, I found this hard to accept because other bulky reports were still intact. All references to the first doctor I had attended in Coventry, who in 1962 had obtained my files from Ireland, were also missing. Determined to obtain my full medical records, I made a series of phone calls to hospitals in Belfast and eventually my completed file proved that I was not and never had been epileptic.

However, I still wonder why I was prescribed Mysoline for seven years with no supervision or subsequent tests to monitor the effect such a tranquillizer was having. I have recently learned that Mysoline is no longer used except in the treatment of epileptic dogs.

I scrutinized the family details I had compiled, a fumble of documents with beautiful-sounding addresses that concentrated my mind's eye. It was with these rummagings and a relentless compulsion to face the past that I decided to return home again. The knowledge that my wife was to accompany me on the week's holiday eased my anxieties. What saddened me most was that it was only because of William's death that I was able to go.

In 1986, after twenty-three years of self-enforced exile, I had returned to County Armagh to make peace with William on his deathbed. Duty done, I had left immediately, the ghosts of my past still too powerful to withstand.

On the plane I had eaten a small Ulster breakfast as if in preparation for my return to this lovely country now synonymous with death and violence. Anxiety wrapped itself around me like too tight a vest. What would it be like? Would I be accepted? I thought of the area so well known to me in childhood: Markethill, Newry, Portadown, Tandragee, Keady, Crossmaglen and Armagh City. Flashes of TV news depicting devastation darted through my mind, reminding me of events during my long absence. How could it all have happened? How had the lush serene country of my childhood become one of the most dangerous places in the world? Most people associate the present troubles with 1969. However, as I mulled over the pages of my mental photo album, an uneasy dawning provoked questions which until now I had conveniently pushed aside. Were the battle-lines drawn during my childhood, placed there carefully like fillets of cement set to withstand future pressures? In my own town of Markethill I remembered the police with guns and the sandbagged barracks. Within the community, fear of an IRA attack was muted, occasionally changing angrily to the 'stupid bastards' when bridges were blown up, blocking lonely country roads.

I remembered the heavily black-clad figure of William, huddled with other B Specials at windy crossroads, when one week after he was transferred from a distant brigade to the convenience of our own townland his old comrades shot dead a man in a car who failed to stop after being signalled to do so. There was my father's disgust at the RUC having to fight battles against men who shot at them from behind hedges two fields away. And the first few lines of a lengthy poem from a book kept in our hall-stand:

> *Shall time erase the memory of the ragmen mean and rough,*
> *Who sought to face our special boys at the school of Mulladuff?*

I thought of the rural disparities and pressures. Not so evident then, they now seemed as stark as the bloody pictures of Christ nailed to the cross.

Religion was fed to us like hot stews to make us grow,

and, commandeered into the Orange Order, we were made to beat triangles, play accordions, and learn the 'Sash', the most famous of all Protestant marching songs.

The jealous guarding of lands that had been in families for generations promoted scorn for those who released territory. I reflected too on the long fierce legal battle with William for my share of the farms.

These memories stormed about my head and I countered the rush with comforting thoughts of home and my reasons for being here.

'Make your peace, say goodbye, and get back on the plane.'

A ginger-haired freckled man, built like a bullock, squeezed himself into the taxi and drove off towards Portadown. The sky was damp, the roads deserted. He didn't talk much and it suited me. Anxiety had left and fear was encroaching. Why could I not be like father or my brother Joe? They were fearless men. I must have inherited my mother's genes. She was shy and timid, and momentarily I hated her.

Already I was clinging to the slippery sides of a tunnel that sucked me back to childhood.

'Come on, come with us, you're ours again, you didn't think we would let you get away, did you?' whispered a voice in my head.

High on a hill, Craigavon Hospital with its glare of windows sat elevated like a half-way heaven. I had spoken to my sister Molly before leaving England so they were expecting me. At reception, a kind-looking woman asked,

'Are you the brother from England?'

'Yes, I am.'

'Well, it's a long way up, take the lift and go to the end of the corridor.'

My breathing was erratic. In a room on the right I saw a huddle of people sitting splay-legged on vinyl seats. At the back two stern-faced young men looked uncomfortable wrapped in outsized green clothes. They stood up quickly, hands concealed, when I came in, then sat down again. My cousin John moved forward and shook my hand.

'How are you, boy?' he asked.

To his left a middle-aged stocky man with thinning black hair and a surprised look nodded and made to stand up.

'William's in there, John,' said my cousin, pointing to an open door.

The room was untidily packed with people I didn't know apart from Violet, the sister I had missed so much. Her black wavy hair had been cut short to her ears. Her small hands were red and chapped.

'John, hello, this is terrible, isn't it?'

I nodded.

'It's good of you to come,' she said.

William lay hunched on a table. He was much bigger than I expected.

'He took a turn yesterday,' whispered Violet. 'They brought him here and now he has gone into a coma – the doctor says it's a tumour on the brain.'

Beneath the window three brow-furrowed women, arms folded, sat on guard. None of them fitted my faint memory of William's slim wife. Scanning them, I asked, 'Which one of you is Sally?'

'I am,' said a sad-faced plump woman.

'Molly not here, Violet?' I asked in a rough voice.

'No, she'll be along later, but have you seen Joe?' she asked, rescuing me from an awkward silence.

Back in the waiting-room I was embarrassed at not recognizing the black-haired man who had earlier made to stand up. It was my other brother.

'Hello, Joe, I thought it was you,' I said shakily.

'Well, I would have known yourself anywhere, John,' and he offered me his seat. After some nervous exchanges, I asked him to introduce me to the bulky green-clad men.

'Ah sure, these boys are not with us, they're just waiting,' he said with surprise.

I later learned that they were armed police guarding an RUC officer who had been shot that morning and was lying in the room next to William.

After lunch I walked aimlessly around the corridors with Violet. My other sister Molly still had not arrived. When Violet left I made my way back to the ward. William's shoulder felt cold and clammy as I whispered 'I forgive you.' He shuddered and snorted, and I felt the words had reached him. Now with his life slowly slipping away, he too forgave. Peace had touched us both, but why did it have to be like this? A current of emotion shook my body – the childhood I had sentenced to dark imprisonment burst back into my brain but my resolve stiffened and I waved a sweeping goodbye to the sea of faces.

Next morning, on the way to the airport, I stopped at the parish church, its squat granite walls as imposing as ever. I walked quietly along a stone path to the graveyard and found the identification plate that had leaned there since 1959. The number 44 barely visible through the rust projected a force so strong it seemed to engulf me. The anonymity of my parents' grave wounded me. Here in a beautiful holy acre of Ireland I saw and felt ugliness.

Two years later, I planned my second return. What would I tell them? They must have known that I parted company earlier with Uncle Joe and lived briefly with Aunt Minnie, father's sister. I would tell them about the lonely years spent in miserable flats, the hunger, the search for security and identity, and the craving for love and affection. I would tell them about my desire to be alone at Christmas despite the occasional invitation to join a family. Of course I would tell them about the struggle for work, my yearning to be accepted as part of society and to achieve total financial independence. I would explain how at twenty I fought off a nervous breakdown, that my wish to become a boxer was halted by the result of another EEG. I would tell them that as I grew older I found opportunities which rewarded my efforts with recognition and stability. I would tell them about my lovely home.

When the time came I said none of these things, my preparatory thoughts were washed away with the warmest welcome I had ever received. Of the seven days spent, five were taken up visiting relatives and friends. They offered us their best chairs, stuffed us with food and begged us to come back. My brother and sisters regarded me with mannerly interest while I scanned them for signs of semblance. Sadly I saw none. I do not think the passage of time had altered them significantly. It was I who had changed, so much so that as I reflected on the lad of Seaboughan Lane, driving home the cows, it was like seeing a mirage.

I found it strange that most people did not mention William other than to say that he had gone home early. I asked my family why, in their opinion, he had beaten me. They didn't seem to know and in quiet moments apologized for what had happened, stressing that they had been unaware it was so serious. For many years I had harboured bitterness towards William for the violence he had inflicted but now I could see it differently. He beat me because of his own frustrations, for a youth lost, plundered by pressure and a responsibility he was unable to bear.

At Glassdrummond Church I gazed at the headstone I had had erected over my parents' grave before filing into the pew to listen to a service that had not changed in twenty-five years.

Reunion with Patsy Goodfellow, my closest childhood friend, was a celebration of a bond of love which time had not eroded. We embraced each other and with my cousin John Hunter spent many hours laughing and reliving a way of life now vanished.

Our farmhouse at Lisnagat lay derelict, a grey ghostly aura shrouding the disfigured main dwelling. A faded curtain flapped through a broken window. The few outbuildings that had not crumbled into heaps of stone were now owned by a neighbouring farmer. The people I spoke to were upset that the fields had gradually been sold off thus landlocking the house, but as I walked through its chilly atmosphere I felt it was what the house wanted. To be left alone forever.

One

I was born on 18 May 1947, the youngest of five children. Our home was near Markethill in County Armagh, a town built not so much on a hill as on a slope. At the bottom of its wide street lay J. D. Hunter's, a general store selling everything from groceries to animal food. Father dealt here, paying the bill on an agreed once-a-year basis. The livestock sales yard next door was a favourite haunt of my brother Joe, who wanted to become an auctioneer. I am sure he would have been suited to the exciting rich language they used to whip up interest in a cow with the worse dose of skitter ever seen.

Opposite the yard, the chemist's roman numeral clock above the door made it the most looked-at shop in the town. Our favourite shop, Boyce's, was in Newry Street, a short walk from the main thoroughfare. Santa must have bought all his sweets there. Gob-stoppers, lollipops, toffees and large untouchable jars crammed with temptation floated colourfully before us through the small window. Old Mrs Boyce used to scrape the bottom of the jars with bony fingers.

'And I'll have a pennyworth of these and twopence worth of those. How much are these ones? No, I'll have them ones.'

'Now, you're having these, John Hughes, and that's it. You've been here for ten minutes,' she'd say.

Back in Main Street the two public houses opposite each other were owned by the Robinson brothers, Louis and Tommy. Years earlier they had quarrelled and still did not speak. Louis was also the local undertaker and word had it that he knew his customers so well that rarely did he have to measure them for their last journey.

At the top of the street, opposite the ever-popular Morgan's Bar, was Jimmy Dixon's barber's shop with its red and white pole outside. If Jimmy was not in his salon we would just wait at the door knowing that he would soon spot us. He'd come tearing across from Morgan's Bar, push his brown horn-rimmed glasses high up on the bridge of his nose, button the white coat and explain, 'Right, boy, I've just been to see a man about a dog. Usual style, is it?'

The question was irrelevant. Jimmy was inflicted with scissoritis so there was only one style – fast and furious. If he'd been to see too many men about too many dogs then it was just furious. As with all the traders in town he liked my father and sometimes slipped me a drop of Silvikrin hair oil. I hated having my hair cut.

'It's too cold for a haircut, Da,' I'd moan.

'You're having a clip or I'll graze you with the sheep. Come on,' and grabbing my elbow he'd steer me in. Hunched like a frightened rabbit I'd endure twenty minutes of incessant snipping. Though Jimmy might pause to greet a customer, the scissors would continue their rhythm around my ears.

'Who's a good-looking lad, then?' father would say when the job was complete.

'He is that, Willie, but keep him covered up for a few days, he might be catchin' cold without all that wool around his ears!'

On the Keady Road out of Markethill lay a small cottage surrounded by black painted sheds and a lovely garden. George Gardner the postman lived here. My father claimed that he was the result of a visit by the Black and Tans to our area and insisted he would look better in a Glengarry than in the old black cap he always wore. Leaning from side to side, with a big brown sack on his back, George's lumbering legs generated just enough power on his ancient bicycle to propel him to the farmhouses along his delivery route.

'*Cuckoo – cuckoo – cuckoo.*'

The sound echoed for miles and everyone knew that George, the man with a hundred clocks in his house, was on his way.

But thirty-five years ago I cared for nothing, beyond the maze of white gravelled roads that led me past farms and cottages, up hills and through peaceful countryside, where cud-chewing Friesians in rolled-back fields clambered up green clumped banks to gaze at me. In blustery showers I would shelter under trees or walk tight against thick hedgerows, shielding my face with a rain-soaked leather satchel. Our home farm in Lisnagat, a rambling old place formerly known as Lisnagat House, had about fifty acres of arable and grazing land. It was approached through a long bumpy lane skirted with hedges and ferns. The house overlooked a bedded stone yard with steps leading down to a sunken terrace and a whitewashed scullery beyond. Cool and airy in the height of summer, it stored our foodstuffs.

Being three miles from Markethill, the farm had no gas or electricity, but the pale moonstone light of the tilley-lamp glowed with a special beauty. It was an art to keep hurricane-lamps alight as we scurried across the windy yard to comfort a calving cow.

There was no indoor lavatory, and if one of the two chamber-pots could not be found, then groping our way down the stairs, along the hallway, and out into the cold rat-infested yard, taught effective bladder control at night.

We grew oats, barley and hay, with potatoes, turnips and other vegetables for our own consumption. The six-hundred-odd poultry, hundred pigs, sixteen sows, herd of white Herefords and seventeen milking cows depleted the food-stocks and kept us hard at it.

My father was both clever and resourceful, building the byres, piggeries, dairy-house and huge hayshed himself. He could mend and make all manner of farm implements and had, as a young man, built a milk cart for his father. He devised a drinking system for the cows by erecting a tall concrete structure around the well. A ladder led to a

11

wooden platform supporting a large tank at the top. From the dark hole the water was pumped up by a diesel generator, through pipes to the cows' drinking bowls. The cows soon learned to activate the supply by pressing their noses against the flanges. None of these skills had been taught. My father studied the problem, decided on a solution, then set about making it work, and it usually did.

Our second farm, called McCune's after its previous owner, was two miles away. Wild overgrown hedges and trees shaded the lonely entrance where the wind was always in conflict with itself, and only the occasional rasp of a corncrake invaded its seclusion. Cattle were sometimes grazed here, and a rusting corrugated metal lean-to provided shelter on rainy days and some protection from tortuous clegs in blistering heat. A five-bar gate opened onto a part-cobbled yard that even sure-footed bullocks were wary of crossing. The house was a grey crumbling ruin flecked with whitewash. The only habitable room served as my grandparents' home. I remember seeing the old woman dressed in black, stick in one hand and a bucket in the other, negotiate her way to the tiny well at the end of the yard. I had visited them once with my father, leaping down from the tractor to chase a three-legged rat. Then, peering into their room, I saw a few sticks of furniture, a mattress on the floor, some bales of hay and bread and jam on a well-scrubbed rough-hewn table.

One day the old lady hobbled the two miles to our house. She said she felt tired, so father told her to go upstairs and lie down. She lay for a week until she died, and I cried every night because she was in my bed. Grandad, who considered himself something of a lay preacher, visited us every month afterwards. 'Don't lose it,' he would say, pressing bright shillings into our hands. I was sad when he died but pleased with the day off school.

Except for a few early Christmases when father was alive, festive occasions passed us by. One day my sisters announced that I would be six tomorrow and that was enough for me. I stood in the front field surrounded by a rush of buttercups, a gentle breeze rocking the sally trees and the apple blossom in the orchard all fluffed up in powdery pinkness. I did not expect presents, but to my surprise Violet gave me a bagful of soft toffees. She rubbed my hair and told me I was a big boy now.

Chewing my last toffee, I watched the cows meander in after milking to graze the long grass. Father had warned me not to trust old Nancy, but I liked her and watched her waddling towards me; slowly at first, then suddenly breaking into a trot, she lowered her head, put her horns down and charged. I panicked and fled. 'Roll, John, roll,' I heard as I tripped and fell. I rolled and thudded into father's feet. There was a sharp crack and Nancy halted, stunned by the blow from his pitchfork. For a few seconds she snorted in defiance, then eyes rolling, tail swishing, she tramped angrily away swinging her head.

'I told you to mind her,' growled father.

My mother was ill for as long as I can remember. Never without a stick, she was unable to walk without leaning on someone. For most of the day she sat in her high-back chair by the range, long black hair hanging over sunken cheeks, her eyes eternally pleading. Brown stockings covered the thin tightly clenched knees. I was sad, but also angry because she could not cook, tidy the house, tie corn or feed the fowl like other mammies.

'Your mammy has paralysis,' I was told, and that was that.

At Sunday school I learned about God and the wonderful things that Jesus could do. He had cured lepers, made cripples walk and blind men see. I desperately wanted mother to walk, and to me the solution was simple; Jesus could help her, so I prayed for many months.

Life on our farm was busy and instructive. We were taught how, but not why. Men must know how to shoot, so with a syrup tin lodged in a tree stump the butt of the shotgun was placed into William's or Joe's shoulder, and father shouted his brief order.

'Hold her tight or she'll kick you, hammer back, aim and pull the trigger.'

William was to become a skilled hunting-and-shooting man, but I remember how he damaged the new gun trying to prevent a wounded rabbit from escaping. Missing the rabbit's head, he cracked the butt on a stone. The beating father gave him was as bad as the one he received for smoking, when he was stripped naked in the bedroom and thrashed with a leather belt. Besides getting shooting instructions, my two brothers were told that they must defend themselves at all costs. To back down was to bring shame, and when Joe blurted out that he had been bullied at school father promptly smacked him around the head, making him promise that he would gain revenge the next day. If he failed William was to take up the challenge and uphold the family name.

Although I hated being the youngest these violent events made me glad that I was not as old as my brothers. Boys more than girls were expected to contribute to farm chores and know how to behave themselves. I did not fulfil these expectations. Not only was I useless at simple chores, I was a cheeky wastrel who wore out boots too quickly and ate too much.

'He's got tapeworms,' my father said.

I knew what these were as the vet used to come to dose the pigs, and wondered if I had just one or a host of them. Comparisons were drawn with male cousins my own age.

'They can drive the tractor, tie corn, milk the cows,' my brothers complained. But mother protested when I was beaten.

My sister Violet and I were to learn how to take care of mother, turning her over in bed to powder her blotched and reddened back. Violet could already cook and made her scrambled eggs and semolina pudding.

Our wonderful neighbours, the Goodfellows, lived just a field away from our farm. Mrs Goodfellow, if she were down early, got me ready for school. In the mornings when I saw her step out on her downhill stroll, I delved into the sink, washed where I thought she would look, then yelled, 'I'm done, Mrs Goodfellow, honest, I am.'

'I'll be the judge of that.'

If a neck-twisting, ear-poking inspection revealed I wasn't then an armlock secured my head, and she gave my face an urgent scrub with a sponge. Mrs Goodfellow was tall and sturdy, with dark hair pinned back with clips, laughing green eyes and a chubby face that showed an earthy kindness. She helped with the washing and cooking, teaching Molly and Violet how to make soda farls and apple pies. At threshing times she organized dinner and tea for about twenty men, but it is for her kindness to my mother that I remember her.

Father marvelled at her enormous capacity for work, and often, to the embarrassment of hired hands, boasted she could make two of any man. She could tie corn with the best of men, feed fowl, prepare eggs, and on potato-lifting days be half-way up a drill with a bag of pinks while others were still tucking in their trouser turn-ups.

This kindly woman had enough to do for her own family and an ageing sick husband. Her home was a tiny two-roomed cottage built of stone, its walls whitewashed to a brilliance that split your eyes on sunny days. Her binder-twine line exhibited a starched array of sheets and shirts that flapped in the wind like loosened tarpaulins. Their only bedroom was partitioned with curtains to provide some privacy. The entire family helped out when needed and without them it would have been very difficult for us to manage.

Father, himself a devilish man, appreciated her mischievousness. Having hinted her intentions to us, on Hallowe'en night, wrapped in a white sheet, she knocked on our door making us squeal with fright. She loved music, and on summer evenings, surrounded by her family, she sat on the gate listening to father play his old button-key accordion until dusk. During this treasured hour father was happy, relaxing his broad, muscle-packed body. His square stern face, normally cracked and furrowed, mellowed to a gentle welcoming smile. How I longed for him to stay this way, not wanting to be scared of that powerful presence which still filled the kitchen, even as the scrunch of his brown hobnailed boots echoed away across the yard.

Two

𝕒

Violet and I walked the one and a half miles to a small country primary school in Cladymore. If it was raining heavily father might tell us to jump in the car; or in the freshness of snow we held on to the wheelguards of the tractor as it crunched deep tracks through the white stillness of the morning, disappointed when he said, 'Right, hop off here, I'll come for you at three.'

The distance children walked to school then is unheard of now but in the rural safety of rutted lanes and fields of the 'fifties it was accepted. When our legs lengthened, bicycles appeared. Scared that the wheels would not keep going in a straight line, it was many months before I ventured beyond a short run on level ground with one foot only on the pedals. With Violet's patient assistance I eventually conquered the red Raleigh flyer that was to become my freedom. Father and my brothers were busy when punctures sank my world and soon I latched on to the kindness of my friend's father. Patsy Goodfellow would shrug off my disasters. 'Ask me Da, he's good at them,' he'd say. Francy Goodfellow became my mechanic, replacing brake pads, fixing lights and, with some reluctance, fitting racing handlebars. Violet, an anxious child, pedalled furiously home from school but I dawdled along the quiet lanes.

From the outside our school looked like one of the many cottages that nestled among wild crimson roses. It was called The Schoolhouse and was a closeted haven of warmth and strength. Not that these humble surroundings did anything to quell my nervous sickness as I rounded the corner of Cladyglen and crossed the bridge. I disliked school and preferred ratting with Spot, my Jack Russell, or stalking the hedgerows weighed down by William's air-rifle, especially at harvest time: those stubble-pricking days spent skipping down the headland to fetch the lemonade bottle, father's Woodbines, or the lunch basket tucked in the hedge.

Miss Clarke, my teacher and headmistress, was an imposing freckle-faced woman with waves of thick red hair. She controlled the class with a low voice and formidable look, her big blue eyes compelling attention. The kitchen was dominated by jolly Mrs Johnson who, unaided, prepared and served dinner for about twenty. Dinner-time, the best part of the day, was uppermost in my mind as I arrived each morning. Mrs Allen's class, nearest the kitchen, taunted us at milk-break.

'We know what's for dinner,' they'd chant.

So did we, savouring the smell of stews and dumplings which we later gulped down before elbowing our way through for seconds that were probably someone else's firsts.

'Sit down, Hughes,' Miss Clarke would bellow, 'you're not at home now,' as I shovelled down my favourite rhubarb crumble. Mrs Johnson's semolina pudding was not tackled with the same enthusiasm; you could trot mice on its thick, lumpy surface. But I am sure attendances were boosted by the ample helpings of tasty food. I could not understand how Miss Clarke could eat vile-smelling mildewed cheese. At home it was orange-coloured in the shape of a brick and wrapped in crinkly paper. One milk-break she caught me staring in disbelief as she munched it with cream crackers. Wagged forward by a big finger I stood timidly before her, waiting for a telling-off. To my surprise she offered me a chunk. I squirmed and shook my head.

'Why not, John?' she challenged with delight.

'It smells of socks, Miss.'

'Go outside and play at once.'

Only in the bleak grey of winter, with the arrival of heavy snowfalls, would there be a noticeable absence of pupils. On these quiet coddling days Miss Clarke would gather the few of us there around the old grey stove and hold us spellbound with Enid Blyton.

My best schoolfriend Ivan Greer was a tall thin boy with brown neatly parted hair. He was a studious lad, always smart and smelling of soap and fresh clothes. His arch-rival Mervyn Baird (nicknamed Isaac) was the school prankster and tough-guy. Isaac's big strength was wrestling and on several occasions he had my friend down in the playground, sitting on his chest and crowing, 'Say you give in, say you give in.'

One dinner-break, when the wiry Isaac forced Ivan to admit defeat yet again, Ivan challenged him.

'Would you like to try it with the fists?'

Isaac accepted, and the following day after dinner we all gathered behind the bicycle-shed and formed a circle around the pugilists. I cheered my mate on as he flashed out his bony arms till eventually his knuckles reddened and cut Isaac's gaunt face.

'Have you had enough, Isaac, or do you want some more?'

'No, you've won.'

They shook on it; Ivan was the better boxer, Isaac the better wrestler, and never again did they fight.

Miss Clarke's passion was for gardening. The girls enjoyed helping but for the lads it was a lark-about, and clumps of earth hurtled across paths and rockeries. Every other week we had to cycle three miles to another school in Markethill for woodwork classes. No one wanted to go when she called out the names one afternoon.

'Mervyn Baird.'

'Flat tyre, Miss.'

'Ivan Greer.'

'Somethin' wrong with my bike, Miss.'

'Willie Clarke.'

'I've got a puncture, Miss.'

'Jacky Riddle.'

'Me chain's broke, Miss.'

'I see, it's a conspiracy.' she remarked grimly.

In retaliation she took the class outside to weed her beloved garden. She was not as graceful as she was kind, and Mervyn, Ivan and myself were caught laughing and giggling at the sight of her bending over revealing big pink bloomers down to her knees.

'Hughes, Greer and Baird, stay behind after school,' she commanded in a disgusted voice. We were given a hundred lines each. 'I must not laugh at the teacher.' I did not see any point in the lines as I already knew I had done wrong and was sorry so I wrote this poem to please her.

> One evening just as it was edging dark,
> Away in the distance I heard a bark,
> Far away the fox did run,
> Not seeing the farmer with his gun.
> Over the hill came pattering feet,
> And then I saw a flock of sheep.
> The gunshot fired and echoed and roared,
> And from the fox the blood it poured.
> The farmer now regrets the day
> That he put poor fox away.
> For the seed he scattered did not yield,
> 'Cos the rabbits they took over the field.

It worked and she forgave me.

On my way to and from school I learned that not all Catholics were as nice as our neighbouring Goodfellows. The three Singer brothers all had black beady eyes and dark cropped hair. Heads down, they shuffled along the grass verge, their faces portraying menace as they rushed across the road and pushed me into the hedge. I had been warned already that some Catholics were bad bastards, Fenians.

At home our chores were waiting. We were responsible for feeding and watering the large poultry stock and after changing out of our school clothes father would snap, 'Never mind your oul homework, get up that field and feed them chickens.'

He swore by Rhode Island Reds, but my sisters and I swore at them. I carried buckets of water from the byre across the fields, swilled out the drinkers, filled them up and watched the hens gargle it down. After I had been to every hen-house I started again and topped them up because if a late-night inspection by father revealed half-empty drinkers, he'd rare up, 'Get out of your bed, you fuckin' wastrel, those hens are chokin'.'

There was no point in saying I'd done them twice. Crack! 'Give me none of your lies,' he'd roar and off I'd go eyes smarting and ears ringing.

I have in mind a picture of my sisters in flowery dresses and wellingtons, anxiously scattering corn in tempting trails as far away as their arms could throw, desperate to stave off a field swarming with brown mottled hens and impatient pullets. The older ones would fly aggressively at the buckets, talons clutching, beaks stabbing. Hysterical twirls and shouts of 'Go away, youse' incensed them to riot. With legs scratched and arms bleeding my sisters would drop the buckets in panic as Molly ran for the yard brush and charged the jostling fowl.

In summertime with feeding over we collected in the eggs from outlying nests. If father was scything a headland and shouted, we trembled in case he had found a nest we hadn't spotted. He'd shake and smell the contents and if they rattled or stank we ran for our lives and found a job he was not expecting us to do, hopeful of avoiding a beating.

We hated Monday and Tuesday evenings and the ritual of egg-washing. Mrs Goodfellow, Molly, Violet and I sat in the scullery surrounded by tin baths full of eggs, washing off the grime with scouring pads and cold water. Then we toasted our fingers back to life over the range and dried and packed the gleaming array. We never tried to get away with any that were not perfectly clean. If father didn't spot them, then J. D. Hunter, the merchant, would, and to embarrass father was to set a fury in him that time could not erase.

Mrs Goodfellow supervised these depressing evenings with humour and determination.

'Molly and me'll do these two big baths, youse two do them buckets.'

If we broke one she had us believe father would be told unless we worked harder.

'By Jaysus, you wait till the man comes in, he'll hear of it.'

'Oh you won't tell him, will you, promise you won't.'

'Well, come and do these then.'

'Please don't make us do them,' we'd plead, shying away from eggs crusted with droppings.

'Right, we'll see what your father says then, here he is now,' and terrified we'd busy ourselves, cleaning off the caked manure. If she caught us floating an egg around the bath she'd slip her hand on top of ours, lean forward, shoot out her false teeth and shriek, making us squeal with delight.

Potatoes were a large part of our crops. After digging and lifting they were transported by tractor and trailer to a building with a galvanized domed roof. Grading, bagging and selling had to be completed before late autumn as this building was used to house hens in deep litter during the winter months.

One day mother asked me to help her out into the back yard. Holding on to me she made her way along the corridor, stopping to lean against the window-ledge over-looking her wild rose garden, through the old abandoned kitchen where she started married life. I tried to guide her past her old pantry, which father had warned us not to let her see. As we approached the red peeling painted door, a pig's snout appeared through the rat-chewed timbers. 'Oh dear, this used to be my place,' she said quietly. 'Let's go to the deep litter house and get a potato, you can boil it for me, John.'

Winter was threatening and a chill wind whistled around the yard whipping up stray wisps of straw. We were getting ready to deep-litter the fowl. A pile of rotting potatoes heaped in a corner ready to boil for the pigs caught her eye and she shook her head. As I led her back to her chair she asked, 'Why do they have to sell them all, John? Sure you'll go and look in the other outhouses. Willie must have kept some for us.' I resolved to take more care of her now.

Religious instruction was fired at me with such ferocity that I began to wrangle with myself about 'yer man' in the sky. It was quite simple, I could not see Him yet I was told He was there and could do wonderful things. What puzzled me most was how could He be everywhere at once and see and hear all? So Ivan and I had a chat about it. I suggested to Ivan that if I were to do something really bad and do it in the dark of one of the pig-houses, surely He wouldn't know about it. Ivan was not so sure and thought He was about somewhere. I decided to put it to the test anyway. Going into an old abandoned pig-house I swore my head off, my reasoning being that if He knew about it He would tell my father, or, worse, William, and that would mean a hiding. In the dark corner, face up against the stones, I whispered quietly, 'William's a fuckin' bastard.'

Nervously I crept round to the front yard. Father and William were sharpening the blades of the mowing machine ready to rid the front field of the gladiator thistles. Neither said a word and my doubts about God increased. Surely, if He was so clever, they would know what I had said and father would 'make hawk's meat' out of me.

I embarked on a series of other tests to find out the truth but would not reveal the results of my trials to anyone for fear of being expelled from Sunday school. I tried tossing a coin three times, heads He was there, tails He was not, but two to one was not convincing enough so I decided to take the best of fifteen. To my astonishment thirteen turned up heads even after jingling the coin around in my hand and tossing as high as I could. I was satisfied. He was there and for weeks I lived in fear of Him telling father or William what I had said in the pig-house.

If I could get high enough up in the sky, there might be a crack somewhere, and I could get through to see Him.

What did He do all day? This sky's a big place. Surely by the time He saw someone do something wrong and got down here it was too late. I decided never again to kill a songbird. I was good with my air-rifle but felt sad and confused when a sparrow or robin fluttered to the ground, blood seeping gently from its beak, heaving its chest and closing its startled eyes.

I still prayed for mother but knew He must be very busy. Further proof of His existence came a few months later. I was told that if a tooth came out and I placed it under a stone the fairies would come and exchange it for money. Molly and Violet told me that God showed the fairies where it was and they came for it during the night. I thought this was stupid. If He had to show the fairies where it was, why did He not do the job himself?

When my first tooth came out I hid it under a stone at the back of the house. No one had seen and next day, before school, I went excitedly to check. There was a shiny six-pence – the final proof and I doubted no more.

Later that summer, as I rode along the end of the lonen, I heard an almighty rumpus coming from the direction of Markethill town. There were people shouting and there seemed to be a lot of excitement. It suddenly occurred to me that God had arrived but I would have to hurry to get Him back to fix mother as I knew everyone else would want Him to do things too. The cycle ride was a fury of excitement. Heart beating madly, I careered down the middle of Finlay's Hill. At the bottom a sharp bend came too quickly, a bank hit me and I flew over the handlebars. He must be there – I wasn't hurt, just my face felt sore. My wheel was buckled but still turned and I was off again and away like the hammers of hell past Shield's Farm, the noise getting louder as I entered Keady Street like a rocket, head down.

I felt scared reminding myself that the Bible said if you believed a mountain would move then so it would. I would tell Him I went to Sunday school and prayed every day. What if He was too busy? I ditched the racer at Morgan's corner pub, ignoring its clatter to the pavement, and joined a large circle of people. Pushing to the front I shouted, 'Lemme in, lemme in.'

What was this? I felt sick and almost cried. An old man, well bent over, with a dirty orange-coloured sash around his neck, was beating a large drum. He stopped as someone thrust a bottle of porter at him. As he tipped the bottle up, the strings of wrinkled flesh tightened on his scrawny neck; the stout bubbled and frothed then blew violently back. A suck and a smack and it was empty.

'By Jaysus, I was in need of that. A couple more and I'll give you the "Sash",' he promised with a drunken swagger.

So finally I knew the truth, there was no God, and began the journey home. As I struggled back up Finlay's steep hill in mindless disbelief, I could just make out an accordion and faint voices singing, 'It is worn and it is torn, Enniskillen and the Boyne.' Back home I told no one of my experience.

'Where have you been?' asked father.

'I wanted to see how fast I could ride to Markethill.'

'What happened to the bike?'

'It hit a bank.'

'I'll look at it tomorrow. If I haven't the time show it to Francy Goodfellow.'

He didn't seem angry.

'Only use it for school, do you hear me now?'

'Yes, Da.'

'What's happenin' in the town?'

'They're playin' drums.'

'Oul eejits. If they had to tie a field of corn they wouldn't be botherin' themselves with the Twelfth.'

Three

❦

I was small for my age but soon got over the disappointment of not growing when I met Gougho, someone I was fond of from our first encounter. Just after my eighth birthday father said he was going to Castleblaney to hire help for work on the farm. I found Gougho chopping with a bill-hook and sweating profusely on a bank overgrown with grass and bloodshot daisies. 'Hello der, young falla,' he said straightening up.

'Are you the man that's going to help my Da?'

'I'm yer very man.'

'What do they call you?' I asked.

'The same as yourself,' he replied, his hazel-coloured eyes sparkling mischievously.

'How did you know my name?'

'Ah well, a fairy told me you're a bit of a lad.'

'What fairy?'

'The one that lives in the tree in Seaboughan Lane.'

'Will you show me it?' I pleaded excitedly.

'Yes, but you mustn't be cuttin' any branches or harm it.'

'I won't, honest. Cross my heart and hope to die. Don't cut the daisies, me Mammy likes them.'

'Jaysus, you've a lot to say for yourself, garcon.'

Gougho did show me the fairy tree and although too young to take an interest in Irish folklore, I peered enchanted into its swirl of thin branches, hopeful of seeing a small delicate figure curled up and asleep. Farm-hands gave this solitary tree a wide berth for to damage it or cut it down was to bring bad luck for countless generations.

Gougho (his real name John McKenna) worked for two pounds a week plus bed and board. He slept in a small room at the top of the stairs overlooking the front yard. He rarely made his bed and his pillow was permanently stained with Brylcreem. With a clogged-up brown comb he swept his hair back into waves like a freshly raked meadow. Although only five feet six inches tall he was fit and very strong. Why the stoutly built little man was called Gougho must surely have been due to William, who nicknamed everyone.

He was obsessed with football which he played for County Monaghan with spectacular results. Never trained, he was able to drive a ball off his wellingtons rocketing it up into the sky, over the house and out of sight. Thursday would see him rush through the milking in order to get out. The byre would not need cleaning as this was a morning job, but it had to be sluiced down or father would rare up. It would have already been agreed that William and Joe would feed the pigs, and father, not a man for going out much, would complete the final job of the day, cooling the milk. I am sure that for him this culmination of the day's work was as soothing as playing his old accordion. With his brown hobnailed boots resting on the trough he sang as he stirred, calmed by the flow of water running around the milk cans.

By this time Gougho would have discarded the wellingtons stuffed with newspaper and donned his blue shiny suit. Sporting a pink shirt and a tie with a knot as big as a turnip he would shuffle into the dairy whistling at the ceiling. Nervous and embarrassed at having interrupted 'The Homes of Donegal' he'd stammer out his request.

'Any chance of a pound in advance, Willie?'

The pound bought him a few stouts at Louis Robinson's pub in Markethill, then at ten o'clock he'd free-wheel down the hill to Mrs Goodfellow's with a large box of Roses chocolates under his arm.

'Do you want to come for a walk, Bridget?' he'd ask anxiously.

'Ah, not tonight, John, there'll be cold dew on those

banks and you could catch your death.'

He continued trying to court Mrs Goodfellow's handsome daughter for years. She was a wily young woman much sought after by local lads. Only once did I see her sharing his topcoat in Marshall's Lane eating Roses chocolates.

Gougho hid his chocolates in the corn heaps and would never admit to buying them for Bridget. We all searched relentlessly, our arms probing the cool golden grain, until one evening we struck gold. Molly loved these luxuries and expertly wrapped small stones to near perfection in the crinkly cellophane paper.

Teasingly, the next day she enquired, 'How's the form with Bridget, John?'

'What's it to you?' he snapped.

Putting on her offended look she retorted, 'Jaysus Christ, I mind the time a person could ask a civil question round here without someone ateing the head off you.'

'Tek that yarn off yer face, Molly Hughes, I never came up the river in a banana boat,' and a flustered Gougho stormed off outside.

After failing with Bridget for many years, he turned his attentions to Anna Mary, an equally attractive younger sister. 'Japers, Anna Mary, what a fine-looking woman you are tonight.'

'Ah will you give over, John.'

'No, I mean it, you'll click at the dance tonight.'

'Click my heels maybe.'

'You mind out, Anna Mary, someone might try to hoist the linens.'

'He'll be a better man than you if he does, John McKenna.'

Gougho was wonderful fun and, whilst we teased him unmercifully, he mostly took it in good part. On a stifling hot summer evening in 1957 I first realized there was an authority other than Miss Clarke and father who had to be obeyed. Two milk churns sat immersed in water in the concrete cooling trough of the dairy. Gougho, having finished brushing down the byre, came in to see father complete his nightly ritual of milk-cooling. Placing the wooden spoon on the shelf, father dipped his hand into the water.

'Feel that, John, you could shave in it.'

'You're right, Willie, and it's going to be a hot oul night,' said Gougho, pinching his sticky shirt.

'If these cans go off a wee bit the creamery will send them back. I'm away to Seaboughan to see the brother. Change that water at about nine o'clock but don't let her run too long, the well is near bottom, and see if you can't catch a drop for the hens.'

'Sound, Willie, sound, I will that. The wee fella can lend me a hand, can't he.'

'Aye.'

'By Christ, if it doesn't rain soon, Willie, we'll be in a quare oul way, them pigs are sucking up water like the divil.'

'Well, I'll say one on Sunday morning,' laughed father.

'Say two while you're at it,' said Gougho, swirling the water around with his small red hand.

After father went to Uncle Joe's I felt a little disappointed that anyone's word other than his carried weight, although I soon forgot it as Gougho and I kicked a ball around the yard bouncing it off the hayshed. Nine o'clock came too soon. 'Come on, garcon.'

As we entered the dairy a rat scurried behind the milk buckets leaving only its tail visible. Gougho raised a finger to silence me then nipped into the byre and came back with a length of wood. Kicking away the buckets with a clatter, he jumped as the rat sprang over his shoulder. He managed to move as if heading a ball, then dropped the wood and ran screaming into the yard.

'Christ, did you see the bastard, he came at me like a cat.' When the colour returned to his face he said, 'Go and see if he's still there, garcon.'

'It's OK, Gougho, he's gone, you're safe,' I laughed.

'It's well for you to laugh, the hure was going to take the throat out of me.'

Father ribbed Gougho for weeks afterwards. 'Let's clean up this oul outhouse, John, but be watching yourself behind them sacks. You never know what's in there.'

None of us appreciated the depth of Gougho's fear of rats, until one day, digging out an old stable that had not been used for years. Father, Gougho, William and Joe tore into a caked heap of manure and straw with shovels and forks.

'Jaysus, a person could choke in here,' moaned Gougho stepping outside to escape the stifling vapours.

At the bottom the wafer-thin layers crumbled to dust and several holes appeared.

'I think a man could do to protect his legs, John,' laughed father, tucking his trouser turn-up into his socks.

'Don't be feared, Willie, they're already protected,' said Gougho, holding up his leg and pointing to the bicycle-clip around his ankle. Standing by the door I grinned as he came out again.

'What's the face for?' he snapped.

'Sure that place is crawling. Even the cats won't go in there, Gougho.'

'Go 'way and make yourself useful, you wee skitter,' and back in he went, working close to the door. Suddenly the floor began to move and cave in. Joe's ankles disappeared and up went the cry as rats, skipping and hopping, broke cover.

'Get back in here, you yellow bastard,' bawled father.

A quivering Gougho charged back in from the yard wielding a spade, shouting as if demented.

'Slow down, you eejit, you almost took my head off,' cried William as Gougho attacked a river of brown rats swarming up the wall.

The affray cured Gougho of his fear and from then on he attacked rats with a savage ferocity. The numbers around the farm became alarming and father resorted to Rodine. The pungent stench from the evil poison hung in the air for days afterwards and had to be dispensed with because of the danger to livestock.

'Why don't you get a dog, Willie,' suggested Jacky Love, our neighbour.

'It's getting a good one, Jacky, I don't want a lodger. There again, if I stuck a tail on McKenna here he would do just as well.'

'You wouldn't be too bad yourself, Willie,' said Gougho and went on to tell Jacky how that very day father had strangled a rat that ran up his leg.

Arriving home from school one evening I found father and Jacky sanding a plank.

'Are you making a slide, Da?' I asked gleefully.

'We are, son, we are that, but it's not for your wee arse though.'

'Why? Who's it for then?'

'The rats,' he laughed as he smeared it with grease. 'Roll that barrel round to the back yard, son.'

Lifting the plank up to a hole between the stones and rafters they wedged the other end into the barrel, now half-full of water.

'Do you think it'll work, Willie?' asked Jacky.,

'Surely it will, they'll come out of that hole on to the plank, and into the water before they know it.'

'Christ, you're a clever man, Willie, if it takes off we'll make a fortune. They'll never sell Rodine again.'

Next morning I accompanied Jacky and father to check their ingenious trap. Only two had met their Waterloo and both men were clearly disappointed. Uncle John Hunter was brought in to view the situation.

'Youse pair of eejits,' he laughed. 'What do you take rats for? Mugs?'

'Jaysus Christ, listen to him, Willie, he's trying to tell us we're surrounded by educated rats,' sniped Jacky.

'They've got more brains than some of the fellas around here,' said uncle, explaining that on their descent the rats probably skipped off.

'Listen to it, Willie, will you,' sneered Jacky, turning to father for support.

'Hold your horses, Jacky, give a man a fair chance, he

31

could have something,' said father.

'Well by Christ, I've heard everything now,' and reluctantly Jacky boxed in the sides of the chute with plywood.

'Right boys, we'll see what the crack's like the morrow,' and uncle bid us goodnight.

Early next morning I followed the three wise men in a quick march to the pig-house.

'Well, what did I tell youse? Look at this!' shouted Uncle John. Father was delighted but Jacky brooded and muttered quietly about coveting another man's ideas. The barrel was dragged to the yard and forty-seven slimy rats were shovelled into the dunkle. As our livestock increased so did the rats. Father insisted he was feeding every rat in Armagh and swore that only the pied piper could help. He arrived in the shape of a Jack Russell terrier named Spot. Smooth-haired, with a penny-size black mark on his rump, black silky ears, black centre-stripe down his face, he stood barely a foot high. He grew into a demon, an assassin that could mark rats like no other dog we had ever seen. We formed a special friendship and father, appointing me as rat-catcher, provided seven gin-traps. I became expert at recognizing fresh runs and setting the vicious sharp-toothed killers. I laid traps twice a night checking at intervals, with Spot always at heel. The death toll impressed father and soon I couldn't close the lid on my red post-office savings tin, crammed with coppers.

Occasionally Spot preferred the fireside kindness of Sam and Ginny McCullogh. If he did not respond to my eager shouts, then calling at their house I would be ever mindful of father's advice.

'They've both got TB so I'm warning you, take no tea or biscuits.'

I felt cruel refusing their hospitality but was scared when the sallow-faced pair, bony frames inclined forward, beckoned me in.

'The kettle's on, son, come on, we're having one.'

'I can't, Da wants the dog, there's rats as big as rabbits in the old kitchen.'

'The Lord will make time for us all one day.'

I had heard this quotation from Sam before. In fact all of Lisnagat heard it on Sunday mornings at the Gospel Hall where he preached his fire and brimstone sermons.

My belief that I had tapeworms stayed with me. At first, feeling scared, I hoped they would go away but after a while I accepted them. Seeing them in the pig manure, I said to Gougho, 'They don't look too bad.'

'Ah well, they're dead those ones.'

'Do they eat much?' I enquired casually.

'Oh a brave bit, I'd say.'

The remark worried me. My family was right, this was the reason for my huge appetite. But how could I be sure that I was getting enough food and the worms were not devouring it all.

On Saturdays, my exclusive day with father, he did the grocery shopping and we all hoped for something special, perhaps frying steak. More often it was bacon or liver with boiled cabbage and potatoes that graced our plates on Sundays.

I sat in the front seat for the journey into town and when we parked in Keady Street he'd say, 'Don't let on to Molly or Violet,' as he slipped me a half-crown.

With a ninepenny seat at the matinée I was left with one and ninepence to gorge myself on apple pie and orange drink. Clarke's picture-house was where I first saw my hero Alan Ladd, the tight-lipped man of *Shane*. Down Main Street, along a concrete yard and through a small brown door, I sat and scratched for hours watching *Apache Drums* or *The Last Train from Gun Hill*.

Alighting into the front seat of the car at five o'clock father would laugh at my sugar-sticky face. 'You won't be wanting the feed tonight, will you?'

Pulling out of J. D. Hunter's yard with all his business transacted, he would drive slowly home enjoying a Woodbine and peppering the walnut dashboard with ant-shaped tobacco spits. Glad that a hard week was over, he'd sing or whistle a reel, relishing the acknowledgment of locals as they nodded or flagged him down to seek advice about building a new byre, or buying a milking machine.

At home my brothers and sisters would peer into the big brown box to see what he had bought. A tin of pork luncheon meat might appear, easily opened with a key attached to an overhang strip. If Molly was not going to the pictures she'd fry a feed. A few of the Goodfellows would come for a game of blind-man's buff, and afterwards we would listen to the top twenty, dancing to 'Scottish Soldier' or 'Wooden Heart'.

Saturday was important to me financially. I had devised several ways of accumulating the half-crown necessary to buy a saving stamp for my post-office book. Gougho or William, who had just begun courting, might want their best shoes polished, or the collar of a drip-dry shirt washed. For shoes I charged a shilling. A shirt washed completely was one and sixpence, but I was prepared to do a deal at two shillings for both if they were done on the same day.

Sometimes, sensing father to be in a good mood, I resorted to begging. If his square face was hard and unsmiling I offered to wash the milk buckets, but if he was whistling a catchy tune I approached him coyly in the dairy.

'If you give me threepence then I'll have one and six and only another bob to go for a new stamp.'

My favourite money-spinner was hunting the faraway hedgerows for discarded lemonade bottles which would not be accepted by J. D. Hunter's unless washed and corked.

Sunday, in contrast, was a dismal day. Other than attending to livestock, no work, play or whistling were the rules of the man with the steel-blue eyes. To disobey him meant a cuff from his granite hand, or worse, a lash from his belt. After Sunday school Violet and I had to endure another hour and a half of the main church service, under the watchful eyes of father in his best black suit. His rule by fear was an unavoidable part of our lives. Everyone but William developed a method of behaviour which minimized their chances of being subjected to his batter-it-into-them belief. Molly adopted the role of daddy's-girl to cover up her casual attitude to farming chores. She made apple tarts, ironed his shirts, polished shoes and told him how nice he looked. Joe used his strength and mental agility to surprise. At his first attempt he drove the tractor and, after only one lesson, sat confidently on the iron seat above the razor-sharp blades of the mowing machine pushing off swathes of hay as neat as ice-cream wafers. At thirteen he could scythe and tie corn as well as any man. At fourteen he had the power and rhythm to stride across a harrowed field with father, spraying corn with a bow fiddle.

Being good was natural to Violet; it complemented her fresh countenance and innocent beauty. If father was cross she protected herself by fading into the background, busying herself with menial household chores or home-work. The quality of her schoolwork was exemplary and her handwriting perfectly crafted. She, unlike me, was eager to attend Sunday school and formed a lasting attachment to the Church.

William set himself up in opposition to father and for this he paid dearly. One evening in Markethill he hurled abuse at father, leaving to visit a neighbour. I was awakened by his pitiful screams in the dead of night as father inflicted his revenge. Being the youngest, I escaped a lot of his harsh-ness, but when my head was smacked I would become utterly confused as two days' previously he would have patted me, saying, 'Who's a good-looking lad?' or let me sit by his knee while he played the accordion at a dance.

I sensed that I was unlike my brothers and sisters and tried hard to cover the difference. One day I asked William why mammy couldn't walk. He informed me bitterly that if my mother had not had me she would have been all right. The remark tormented me because I didn't know where babies came from and constantly wondered how I had made her so ill. Amidst this turmoil I realized my family were aware of the difference and I felt fearfully exposed.

At ten years of age my responsibilities were growing with me. One of my jobs was to fetch the cows home for milking, learning from Joe as we went along the stretch of Seaboughan Lane that spanned the fields and farm. After a couple of months I was trusted to do the job alone and set off early along this enchanted way to the sound of William's shout, 'Don't be all day with them cows, Lippy.'

He nicknamed me Lippy because when he hit me my bottom lip would drop tearfully. For a while I was affection-ately known as 'Bat', I think after a 'comic' character.

Seaboughan Lane was my haven. From a gentle decline, ash trees in high hedges fringed with spongy moss gave way to thicket hawthorns adorned with daisies and dandelions. Willy-wagtails flitted above the flat naturally formed stone path, never letting me come close as they skimmed their way through a crazy dance pattern. Yellowhammers min-gled with upturned bluetits, defiantly ignoring the noisy marriage ceremonies of cackling magpies. Stalking quietly one afternoon with my weak-springed Diana air-rifle, I approached the swollen river and saw trout lying quietly in the black deep holes around the edges. A heron startled me when I advanced in a none-too-quiet manner. Over the river creeping silently, I checked the large meadow on the right. Parting the foxgloves with the barrel of my gun, I tried to ambush a pigeon sitting on the hay waves, the crack discharging panic around the sanctuary. Nervous yellow-beaked moorhens ran head-down to the river's foliage; grey-backed crows flapped hurriedly away from surveillance points; white bobtails hopped into hedges; a covey of partridge hung low then angled through a gap in the oaks; a dog fox, stealthily intent, slunk away in the same direction as a strutting cock-pheasant.

Further on I stopped and leaned my gun against a sally tree, climbing up the mossy bank to look out across Henry Clarke's big field. A large brown hare hammered away to safety under a broken five-bar gate.

'Lippy, come home with them cows,' roared William.

I flew over the whin-bushes, thistles ripping at my

wellingtons, and shouted at the cows outlying in the boundary field. Breaking off a young branch I urged them into the lane for the journey home. Some wanted to stop and skitter.

'You'll have to do it as you go,' I shouted, lashing their behinds.

I was furious. The little meadow was full of things to shoot and all in range. Hot and anxious I lashed the cows again. Wild-eyed they charged along crunching up the brown track.

'Jaysus, I'd better slow down, the steam's rising out of them,' I murmured.

I slipped the gun into the hedge hoping for a shot later.

'Where the fuckin' hell have you been, I'm going out tonight,' snapped William.

'Sorry,' I said quietly.

'You're sorry, my arse. You've been shooting and rushed these cows home. Look at the rip in old Willow's belly, she's been caught with a thorn.'

'Shall I polish your shoes for you?'

'Yes, after you've finished filling the drinkers in the top hen-house, Bat. Where's the gun?'

'In the hedge. Can I go back for it?'

'Aye, but don't be all night in that meadow.'

On a brown autumn afternoon in 1957, father, Gougho, William, Joe and I had turned up half the potato field when an empty drill was uncovered. Father's face was stern as the small tractor shuddered to a halt. Jumping off he took a long look down the drill before joining us for tea and corned beef sandwiches. Gougho looked at father's forlorn face and passed him an enamel mug brimming with tea.

'You'll feel better with that down you, Willie.'

'I'd feel better if that drill had spuds in it,' he replied.

Gougho slurped his tea and with a pensive voice turned again to father. 'I think that one's for your missus, Willie. Let's hope there isn't another alongside it.'

'God forbid, don't say that,' said father, climbing slowly

back onto the tractor.

One hand steering, he gazed back with a faraway look as the next drill too proved empty. The remainder of the day passed on in silence.

Four

❧

Despite my mother's obvious discomfort she frequently enquired about my progress at school.

'Are any of you big ones helping that child with his homework?' she'd ask.

Over my climbing years I watched her state worsen. The hobbling walk with a stick and the desperate grip on someone's arm passed and the bedridden stage arrived. She was consoled by the move downstairs to the sitting-room where she could hear and see much more of what was going on and the open fire cheered her. It also meant that father did not have to carry her upstairs each night, watching her bow and shake her head. Violet and I became strangely synchronized in our moods. At dusk, pushing each other in a wheelbarrow over humps and bumps, we'd stop our jaunts.

'Shall we go and see does Mammy want anything?'

We'd trip in with cups of tea, buttermilk, bread and jam, and the now necessary sleeping tablets. Sometimes I watched my sisters at bedpan duties, wanting to help but turning away in embarrassment from so much pain. It was too far to carry her to the corrugated shack built over a shuck on the far side of the back yard.

The doctor called with depressing monotony to give her the injection that relieved the pain. Violet helped Molly to wash her, but she responded most to Mrs Goodfellow. On one of these occasions I received a shock still vivid in my memory. Walking into the room unannounced, I saw Mrs

Goodfellow washing her. She was naked. I had never seen anyone without clothes on and panicked at the sight of hair at the top of her legs. She tried to cover herself but, horrified, I ran out into the back yard wondering if this was the reason for her illness. The facts of life were only slowly revealing themselves to me and I still did not know where babies came from. When I asked my cousin John Hunter he told me, 'You have to go to Belfast hospital and pick one.'

'Well, how do Mammies pick brothers and sisters to look alike?' I enquired.

'Sure I don't know everything, boy.'

At school Ivan Greer gave me the facts. 'Your Da does to your Ma what the bull does to the cow.'

I was disgusted and thought about it all the way home. In the kitchen Violet was peeling potatoes and I nervously informed her of my discovery.

'Huh! That's news to me,' she said with a sniff.

Mother's condition worsened rapidly. She was often delirious and I listened fearfully to her odd rantings till she fell asleep. One evening she asked me for a cup of water, saying she was in pain and wanted to take her sleeping tablets earlier. I stood by the bedside and watched her fumbling. She swallowed desperately and then told me she wanted to die.

'I have asked your father to choke me; he says he would but they would find out and hang him.'

Her remarks did not upset me at the time, in fact I remember thinking it would be best for her to die if she was in so much pain. Only years later when I discovered that she had died of toxaemia due to disseminated sclerosis did I appreciate the extent of her suffering. Her bedsores became a festering mess, needing constant attention. Grandma Feely and the two uncles, Robert and Samuel, visited regularly on Sunday afternoons. Rushing into the house I'd bawl, 'Mammy, the Feelys are here.'

Her face would light up as she tried to raise herself in greeting. They took her to their farm in Crossmaglen for a holiday twice a year. Late one summer evening, I watched them lift her, crying, into the car.

'Where is Mammy going?' I asked.

'Grandma's.'

'When will she be back?'

'You can come and see her soon, John,' Grandma assured me, patting my head.

They reversed from the side of the overhanging chestnut tree and I ran alongside. The car pulled away and I heard her weak call, 'Look after that child.'

I waved. She turned a little, waved back. I never saw her again.

On Sundays father took William and Joe, or Molly and Violet to see her. He promised to take me soon, but he never did. Looking back I think he did not want me to see her terrible state.

Early one August morning I heard noises and voices in the yard. Stumbling to the window I peered out, my eyes still full of sleep, just in time to catch sight of the car disappearing from the yard. Without any commotion or the normal noisy wakening, everyone rose at seven. A sea-blue sky spanned the horizon promising a warm day.

'Where's the oul fella?' asked William.

'Away to Crossmaglen,' replied a white-faced Molly. 'Uncle Robbie came for him. It was only four o'clock, she mustn't be in too good a form.'

That morning we hardly spoke. Violet and Molly baked bread. The dough was kneaded and kneaded. There would be no sharp surprise of soda in the mouth this time. Locks of hair covered their faces – with only the odd sniffle or open-mouthed glance to the yard expressing their anxiety. William and Joe finished the milking early, rewarded with an extra bucketful each for their fierce tugging.

Sitting on the concrete plinth by the coal-heap I threw stones at a diesel-soaked piece of timber beneath the green fuel tank. At ten o'clock the car came slowly along the lane then rolled to a halt in the yard. Father sat a moment, opened the door and leaned back. I looked directly into the grey face. It was usually difficult to stare at him; his hard ened look melted my resolve, but this morning was different. His cracked face was set and vacant, the cut of his lips turned into his teeth like a snapped rat trap. Walking slowly and stiffly, he surveyed us, then quietly said, 'It's all over.'

He described how ill and delirious she had been, rambling about boots in the window before rallying briefly to ask him to leave the room while she counted them. He had walked to the door and slammed it pretending to leave. She named all five children, then passed away.

'Stop bubbling,' he snapped as Molly sobbed.

I walked around to the deep litter house where we had once searched for potatoes. I was sad yet relieved. She was alright now and I thought about God again, hoping her belief had taken her to heaven.

Mrs Goodfellow papered the back room, distempered the corridor and whitewashed the scullery in preparation for the wake.

Why was everyone drinking whiskey, I wondered? Were they not sad that mammy was dead? And someone was playing an accordion. I was sent to bed at twelve o'clock and tried to sleep. My mind wandered back to the night Violet and I slept together in this room and heard scraping and gnawing beneath the bed. Our terrified screams had brought father with a tilley-lamp.

'Da, there's something under the bed,' we hissed.

'Lie still, I'll be back in a minute,' he said.

When he returned he slid a rat trap under the bed, assuring us it would be alright now. Awakened by the squeal of the rat we squealed too and father came again. 'Go back to sleep now, there's no more rats.'

As the wake continued into the early hours I heard noises in the yard. Buckets and milk churns were rattling around yet there was no wind or rain. Moving towards the window I heard soft singing like a choir, then a low wailing sound. A slim face appeared at the window shrouded in white with a woman's features and a kind expression, stayed a short while, then faded away. Getting back into bed, I curled into a ball and pulled the covers over my head.

Five

The winding country lanes led Violet and me back to school. I was relieved that mother had died during the holidays so that I did not have to suffer the questions of other children.

'Come on, John, we're late,' said Violet, tugging my arm. Round the next corner I was filled with dread as the Singer brothers advanced grinning. Jaysus, there were five of them now! Where had the other two come from?

'Leave John alone or I'll tell my Da on you,' warned Violet, putting herself between me and them.

Miss Clarke was waiting in the flagstoned hallway. She made nothing of my mother's death and I felt excited when she told us we were having a school concert.

Molly had moved to a school in Markethill now. One evening, while she was toasting her legs by the range, father noticed red welts on her thighs. She wrapped the grey skirt tightly around her.

'How did you get those? Well, come on, tell me,' he demanded.

Molly began to cry.

'Stop your snivelling or I'll give you something to cry for.'

She blurted out how she had been larking about in class and the teacher had beaten her with a pointer.

'By Christ, no one's going to bate a child of mine,' father roared. 'You go to school tomorrow and keep your lip buttoned.'

Next evening Molly told us what had happened. She

43

suspected that he would turn up but even she was nervous as the hobnailed boots hammered along the tiled corridor. Banging on the headmaster's door, he stormed in.

'Where's Molly's teacher?'

'Down the corridor, third door on the right,' came the startled reply.

Suddenly a pupil burst into the classroom shouting, 'Sir, Willie Hughes is here, Willie Hughes is here,' as the sound of his big boots advanced again. Molly said the teacher ordered the bigger lads to push against the door while he grabbed his pointer and stood trembling by his desk.

'Who is it?' he asked as the doorknob turned.

'Willie Hughes.'

'What do you want?'

'Open the door or it'll go in.'

The lads were ordered back to their seats and in walked father, his cold eyes staring. Grabbing the pointer, he snapped it across his knee then handed back the pieces.

'That's what'll happen to you if you touch any of my children again,' he said, and walked out.

Molly could make a cat laugh and frequently landed Violet and me in trouble. Meals were taken in silence, not only for discipline, but so father could listen to the news. Intent on hearing about Khrushchev or the latest with Nasser and the Suez Canal crisis, he never missed the six o'clock broadcast. While we sat around the table, Molly pulled faces and when father flashed his sobering looks her face was straight and we were still giggling.

William and Joe sometimes skipped tea, as the quiet dusk was perfect for rabbit shooting. Myxomatosis, with the carnage it brought, had not reached us yet. How could we have envisaged rabbits in hundreds stumbling blindly over roads and fields, pus oozing from their closing bulbous eyes? William, a hardened hunter, was sickened later at having to dispatch so many with a blackthorn stick since cartridges could not be wasted on unprofitable kills.

I remember my first encounter with the effects of the

cruel disease. One morning, peeping through a gap in the hedge, I scoured the sweep of our front field down to the nettle bank. Body pumping with excitement I tore home.

'Da, all the rabbits are out and just sitting there!'

'How many's out?'

'Hundreds of them, honestly, you can't see the grass.'

'Go and tell William, I've got to get this tractor started,' he said.

William hastily threw me a sack.

'Come on, before they go.'

'They're everywhere, William, big as hares and just sitting there.'

'Alright, button your lip. You'll grow up to be a preacher with a mouth like that.'

'Just you look through here,' I said, crouching by the hedge.

'Holy Christ, you're right, boy. Get down.'

'Go on, shoot, William.'

'No, I want two together, the oul fella's short of cartridges.'

He slid the gun through the leaves, and globules of morning dew teared on the barrel. A deafening bang echoed in the hollow and faded across the field.

'Jaysus, I've got them both,' he cried. 'Give me them cartridges.'

'They're not running away,' I said in amazement.

William looked puzzled and, grabbing a knotted branch, yanked himself up on the bank. Smoke coiled from the end of the gun barrel as he stared around.

'By Jaysus, I've never seen that before.'

As we tramped across the damp grass, startled rabbits hopped about and ran blindly in circles.

'Christ, it's here,' he said.

'What is, William?'

'Myxomatosis, the oul fella said it would reach us.'

Before this William had made good pocket money. A cleanly killed rabbit fetched two shillings, grey-backed crows half a crown, and a fox's tongue, taken to the police station, was worth ten shillings. Crawling on his belly, William could easily get to within ten yards of a rabbit. Bow and arrow, catapult, or spears made from brush-handles: he was deadly.

The Marshall brothers, James, Bertie and Willie, living a mile away from us, were handy with snares, a practice denied William and Joe as father forbade their use on our land. When they proposed a partnership in spoils, my brothers gladly accepted. An abandoned ten-acre farm adjacent to our front field was selected as the hunting ground. Andy Anderson, the owner, only used it to graze cattle or cut hay, and soon my brothers learned the ways of snaring. The agreement was for all to meet early in the morning before milking to collect the bag, but William had other ideas. 'Come on, Bat, wake up, here's your shirt,' he whispered one morning.

'Where's my wellies and trousers?'

'You don't need them. I'll carry you. Now shush, the oul fella will kill me if he hears us.'

We stole quietly down the stairs and out into the yard. Dawn was breaking.

'Here, Bat, hang on to these corn sacks.'

Shivering I alighted on his back like a cleg on a cow, and with my bare arse to the wind away we went, keeping to the headland to avoid thistles and the tell-tale yellow seeds of ragweed.

'Will you sit up a bit, you're choking me,' he gasped and shunted me further up his back. At the barbed wire fence he perched me on a post, climbed over, then lifted me down.

'Jaysus, will youse look at them,' he said.

Most of the snares were full and, after breaking the necks of those caught by their legs, he reset the wires.

'Get up that tree and shake like blazes, Bat.'

I carried the apples, he the rabbits. Where he had left footprints in the dew he raked the grass with his hand. Back home, the sacks hidden in the barn, we crept back to bed. Gulping down his tea at breakfast William announced, 'I'm just going to check the snares with the Marshalls.'

Soon he was back.

'Did you catch anything, son?'

'No, Da, they were all empty.'

'I didn't think you'd do any good, shooting's the only way. I'm away to the Marshalls' bull now,' he said, scraping back his chair.

Walking a wild-eyed cow to a bull along two miles of winding roads could prove an ordeal for the best of cattlemen. Father was aggrieved at paying a pound for the service, but since the Marshalls owned the only licensed bull in the area he had no choice. Spring that year brought the calving of a fine-looking beast that grew into a powerful red charger. Word soon got around what a beauty he was, and before long the clatter of hooves could be heard along our lane. When father and my brothers were out Molly was left in charge.

'Did he manage? Was everything OK?' she would ask, clutching the dirty ten-shilling note.

'Willie, I haven't come to cause you any harm, but have you an unlicensed bull?' asked Constable Bertie Henry after his three-mile jaunt out from the sandbagged barracks in Markethill.

'Well, I might have, but then again, I might not have.'

'Look, we've had a letter in about you,' Bertie confessed. 'It says you have an unlicensed bull roaming wild with the cows in Seaboughan Lane.'

'But sure ours are the only cows in Seaboughan Lane,' replied father, 'I own most of the land.'

'Now look, Willie, there are other cows in the fields near the lane, but in any case, that makes no difference. Have you an unlicensed bull or haven't you?'

'Give us a luk at that letter.'

'Now you know I can't do that.'

'Well, I'll do a deal with you, Bertie. Hold up the letter and let me see the handwriting and I'll make your job easy for you.'

Carefully concealing the address and the signature, the Constable held up the letter. Father smiled, recognizing Mrs Marshall's writing.

'Fair enough, I've got a bull.'

In court, father's lame excuse that it was too cold to castrate was dismissed. He paid his fine and the bull was sent to market, but that was not the end of the affair. That evening at tea-time I watched as he drummed his hard fingers on the table.

'The shower of dirty bastards. Prigs of the first water, that's all they are. Well by Jaysus, I'm not having it. Gemme that paper.'

He scanned the *Armagh Gazette*. 'Thought so! I'll have the hures. It's Balmoral next week. You can come with me,' he said, winking at Joe.

'We're not having another bull, are we, Da?'

'We are son, we are at that, even if it breaks me.'

The third-prize winner, a giant white Hereford, was dropped off at Markethill. Walked noisily home by father and Joe, every quarter of a mile or so farmers appeared to see what all the commotion was about.

'By Jaysus, Willie, it'll be a few quid to take a cow to that fella?'

'Not at all, I'm not a greedy man, ten bob'll do and you can call any time. If I'm not in, he'll be in the front field and one of the childer will be about.'

But after mother's death father gradually lost heart. He had never drunk alcohol and was scornful of those who did, yet now he went out on the occasional binge. I used to wonder why he took Joe with him, but looking back I think he sensed his own vulnerability and knew that Joe was strong and powerful enough to deal with any trouble he might lead them into.

I lay awake during these long nights waiting for the sound of the car. When he came home he gave me a bottle of porter or lager. It tasted foul but I drank it to please him. His flagging in the farm meant that William and Joe had to work harder, harvesting, milking, feeding pigs and poultry – but they took it all in their stride. Only in the ploughing season did his interest revive and he worked from morning till night.

'Sure that man will kill himself yet,' said Uncle Joe Hughes, as he watched him furrowing Seaboughan hills with only the tractor lights for guidance. Uncle eventually gave up what he called 'dirt scratching' and, after auctioning off his farm and machinery, he took his wife and family over to England. His departure meant father lost the alibis his brother often provided to explain the increase in our pig stock.

I am sure de Valera's government did not object to pigs being smuggled into what they considered to be the richer six counties. The northern farmers paid more than their own market price so they must have been well pleased with the deal. The greatest problem was getting past the border check near Crossmaglen on the way home from Castleblaney, but on the promise of a luck-penny from my father, the pigs were delivered.

There was an added bonus to these excursions for which the help of Molly was enlisted. Male guards at the border could not search females so, with her knickers stuffed with Sweet Afton cigarettes, she sat like a queen in the front seat.

While I was sweeping the yard one morning an old blue van hand-braked to a halt in the yard. 'Where's your Da, son?' a stranger enquired as the engine throbbed.

'Up by the barn,' I said. There he was, scouring the lanes with William's small binoculars.

Around the back the van doors were opened and a litter of young pigs slid about, their trotters catching in the floor, which was slatted to prevent leg breakage. Gougho grabbed one and carried it squealing across the yard.

'Sure they're a load of skittery-arsed hures, these are, Willie,' he said, eyeing them critically.

'Ach, they'll be alright with some dry meal and spuds inside them.'

Next day a black car suddenly sharked into the yard, then skidded to a halt, catapulting gravel against the shed. Flinging open the doors two men piled out, one heading towards the piggery, the other to the house.

'Police, Da, police,' yelled Molly, grabbing a chair to

reach the Sweet Afton from the shelf high above the range.

'Molly, don't forget my tay,' father hissed as he crept down the hall and out into the back yard, eyes darting, before slipping away down Seaboughan Lane.

Molly was ready, one hand on the latch of the half-opened door.

'My Da's not in.'

'Well, go and ask him when he will be in.'

'Sure I've told you he's out somewhere.'

'When will he be back?'

'How would I know, it's none of my business, I feed the hens.'

'Give me none of your lip, Molly Hughes,' said the policeman, and off he went to the barn to stand on the top of the coal heap, scouring Seaboughan fields with field-glasses. William watched, hands thrust deep in his dunga-rees.

'Hello, Sur, it's a fine mornin'.'

'It would be better if we could talk to your Da. Has he bought any pigs recently?'

'I know nothin', seen nothin' and heard nothin'.'

'You're one of the Hugheses alright, you are,' and he stormed back to the car. Slamming the doors they screeched off in a cloud of dust.

By now, father had reached the two big ivies at the end of Seaboughan Lane. After a smoke he crawled along the deep ditch encased with briars and nettles until he reached Uncle Joe's.

'Can one of your sows stand for ten pigs, Joe?'

'I'm afraid not, Willie. One's got a litter with her and the other two are due to pig in a month's time, but hold your horses and I'll let you know in a while.'

Back in the briars, father made his way down to the ivies. Soon Molly sauntered by, whistling, stopped beyond the hiding-place and tucked a basket into the ditch.

'They've gone from the yard, Da, but they have the glasses on the fields,' she whispered.

'Did you bring me a blanket?'

'Yes, it's under the kettle at the bottom.'

'Good girl. I don't know how long Joe will be.'

Eventually Uncle Joe arrived back with the name of a man willing to swear that his sow had reared the Landrace-lookalikes in our piggery.

Six

ᘔ

Father enjoyed pig farming but what happened next depleted his already flagging morale. Our pigs were affected by a rasping cough and we were devastated one morning to find two bluish corpses in the pig-house. Vercers, the knackermen, were called and while the high-sided wagon waited in the yard I looked in and saw the bodies of sheep, pigs, a cow, and a big black dog, too young to die.

'Where are they, Willie?' a stone-faced man asked casually.

'Where do you think? Out in the yard.'

With a dejected look father thrust a wrinkled ten-shilling note into his pocket.

'Holy Jaysus, and to think yesterday they were worth twenty quid. I'm in the town the morrow so I'll see what yer man has to say about it.'

The vet brought powder for us to spray on the floors and walls. We disinfected the drinkers and feeders but it was no use. After two weeks and more deaths, the vet was called again.

'I'm sorry, Willie, it's viral pneumonia. They'll all have to go.'

Sadly I watched the wagons being loaded. Father's face tightened and he was silent for the rest of the day.

I enjoyed feeding and watering duties even though I'd never mastered the art of preventing pigs from violently nudging the buckets out of my grasp. I knew I would miss the clumsy creatures but at least there would be no more home killing. The man specializing in this slaughter was evil-looking, with a red whiskey-drinker's face, small eyes and a sinister grin made worse by a hare-lip. My skin crawled as I watched him sharpen the long thin knives, then pull on blood-stained shiny brown trousers matted with small white hairs. Squealing pigs were dragged stiff-legged across the yard, then smashed on the head with a sledge-hammer. As the poor animals lay twitching on the ground a long knife cut the throat and pierced the heart. Blood gurgled out and swam over the concrete, making Violet and me cry hysterically. Often from our lofty height in an old barn we hurled potatoes at the vile man until we were chased away by father.

Taking a pot-shot at crows and rabbits seemed acceptable but the butchery of pigs or the drowning of new-born kittens made me howl with pity.

I was beginning to outgrow the protective sack of childhood and knew that as I got older I too would be expected to take part in the slaughter. I wrestled with myself a long time before testing how much suffering I could inflict. One day I received a vicious stab on my hand from a crotchety Rhode Island Red determined not to be dislodged from its laying-box. Here was a chance to explore how much brutality I could mete out. I even managed to convince myself that this hen deserved to be punished. Taking the wretched squawker into the yard I poured bucket after bucket of water over her until she folded into the ground. Crying with remorse I bundled her into my arms and sat by the range stroking her feathers until she moved her head and cocked a hapless eye at me. I put her back in the laying-box, returning each day to feed her with corn. The incident saddened me, reinforcing my feeling that I could never become a farmer.

The methods used to dispatch livestock seemed barbaric at the time but they were all farmers could afford. The words 'organic' and 'free-range' were not mentioned, they were practised. Animals were well fed, given light and freedom of movement before they met with the swift precision of the travelling executioner.

Father knew I was soft and one morning he ordered me down to the store-house beside the dairy to investigate the racket going on inside. Gingerly I opened the door and a black and white fluffy ball hurled itself at my knees. Father had bought me a pup.

'It's yours, son,' he said. 'We'll call him Shep.'

Spot was around occasionally but now spent most of his time at the end of the lane with Sam McCullogh. Shep grew into a big robust collie and was never far from my heels. I fed him as best I could, giving him some of my own food mixed with old spuds. He too learned to kill rats, but was much more adept at breaking up livestock when rows broke out in the enclosure. I made sure he knew the rules of obedience as I did not want him to irritate father.

After the loss of our pigs we began sheep farming. Come lambing season my brothers took it in turns to sit night-guard against foxes, with the shotgun or the ·22 rifle, acquired through Pat Brady, a devious man not entirely trusted by my father. I think he suspected that Pat was an IRA sympathizer, his distrust deepening when Pat arrived at the farm with a pistol and ammunition, saying he wanted to dispose of them. William was delighted to accept; however, father disapproved.

'You can keep the ·22 but bury the rest,' he said, so William buried the brown steel box by the fox warrens.

Pat's favourite trick sickened us all. In the top pocket of his blazer he kept a small pair of scissors and, on finding young frogs in the damp orchard grass, he held them above his cavernous mouth, snipped off the legs and swallowed. Unable to detect his sleight of hand, we believed he had devoured them, and Molly cringed.

'You dirty oul hure. Tom the devil himself is in you.'

Undoubtedly, Pat was the strongest man we had ever seen. Even father admired his feat with a cart-wheel lapped in a steel band which he'd lift onto the cleft of his chin; he would trot around the yard, hands by his side, while

Gougho collected half-crowns from incredulous strangers.

I am sure given the chance William could have been an Olympic marksman. Father, not a man for compliments, marvelled at his extraordinary skills. Standing back at twenty yards, using my old air-rifle without the refinement of telescopic sight, William split matches and could hit a threepenny piece sideways on. The best shot I ever saw him take was from our back bedroom window, killing a crow on a sheep's head two hundred yards away. Father rared up.

'Don't do that again, you could have killed the sheep.'

He had to smile when William, deeply offended, asked, 'How do you make that out, Da? I wasn't aiming at the frigging sheep!'

His fascination with guns grew stronger and it came as no surprise to the family when he joined the B Specials. With the IRA blowing up bridges, our townland became quietly alert to strangers.

Sunday 29 March 1959 began like any other. After milking we fed the fowl and filled the bellies of one or two roaring calves with milk. A winter sun penetrated the overcast sky as Violet and I cycled to Sunday school. We were pleased at not having to endure the main church service afterwards.

After dinner no one seemed to have any plans for going out. Father sat on the sofa with Molly and Violet. William, now permitted to read the *News of the World*, did not want to come with Joe and me to luk the sheep at McCune's. At the top of the lane we pulled the car onto a frost-hardened standing of earth. Neither one of us spoke much as we wandered about.

'I think they're all here,' said Joe. 'Come on, we'll go.'

Turning into our lane we caught sight of Uncle John Hughes's old black Vauxhall disappearing around the corner. He pulled his car up on the slope in the shade of the chestnut tree. If it would not start later we would push him down past the back yard and away he would roar, waving and grinning. As he walked across the yard to greet us William rushed out, shouting in panic.

'Uncle John, come quick, there's something wrong with my Da.'

'What? What sort of something?'

Racing into the kitchen, a white and trembling Molly said, 'He's on the landing.'

He lay on his back outside the bedroom, with two pillows under his head, snoring loudly. Kneeling down beside him uncle looked perplexed.

'It looks bad to me, William, what happened?'

'He was on the sofa and complained that he had pains in his chest and was going to lie on the bed. Then we heard a thump and I've just found him here.'

William ordered me downstairs where Molly and Violet were sobbing. Later I was told that as William picked him up to put him on the bed he passed away in his arms. At forty-eight years of age, the hard man of Lisnagat was dead. Total disbelief prevailed all afternoon and evening. William looked up into the sky and shouted, 'Is there a man up there at all?'

I went out into the rear yard. After a while I came back through the old abandoned kitchen and crept quietly up the stairs and along the landing to the door of father's room. I turned the knob but could not go in.

Molly told us in a choked voice that only the week before father had taken off his shirt and revealed discoloured lumps around his midriff. She had begged him to go to the doctor but, always stubborn, he had refused.

'It can't have happened,' she wailed. 'Mammy died only seven months ago.'

William muttered something about two rows of unseeded potatoes and I remembered Gougho's comment in the potato field just before mother's death.

Soon the yard was full of people. Mrs Goodfellow refused to believe it.

'Sure he was so young and May died at only forty-five. Why do the good ones have to go first?'

The Hunters took Violet and me to their home, Sweet Briar Farm. All our cousins cried continually asking each other, 'How could the good Lord take him away?'

I was tempted to say it was rubbish, He was not there, I had proved it; but I was too scared. They were big church-goers.

'I can't believe it, not Uncle Willie, he was so strong and I was only talking to him in Markethill a few days ago,' sobbed my cousin Betty.

It was school holidays again and we were to stay for a week until the funeral was over. The following morning Aunt Ruth returned to Lisnagat with Betty.

'Come on, let's go and clean out the house for the funeral,' she said.

Both the words and actions upset us. Powerful in mind and body, kindness her only intent, she organized us with ruthless efficiency. The word 'can't' had no meaning for her.

'Can't, my arse, course you can,' she'd say, rolling up her sleeves impatiently and doing it herself. No one stood in the way of her determination that all should succeed to the best of their abilities. I sensed my cousins' surprise that, unlike them, I was not outwardly upset. Cousin John was most affected, saying how much he loved Uncle Willie.

I liked being at the Hunters; they had electric lights powered by a generator, lots of food, hot water, a bath, and ducks and geese. They also had two sheepdogs, one called Jessie. Nipping at their legs, she could round up sheep much faster than I could. There were two tractors, and a threshing machine in the shed. Cousin John could drive the tractors, and he let me have a go.

'Can't you drive yet, boy? Come on, I'll show you. I can cut corn as well.'

I knew this, having often watched enviously when he was held up as a shining example. I was thrilled. Lippy was driving a tractor and I felt very important.

'Come on, wee John, you can sit on the Fordson Major as well.'

According to John this was the strongest tractor in Armagh. The awesome giant with its deafening sound was used to drive the threshing machine. Proudly he explained how it had been used to pull out large tree roots when the road close to their farm entrance had almost collapsed. He had noticed foxes at the bottom of the sloping embankment and, after telling his older brother Robert, the two boys went with their father to investigate.

'And I was right, boy! There were fox-holes by the dozen.'

His father had the road repaired and congratulated his son for being so observant, saying, 'I'm glad my youngster saw it, someone could have got hurt if it had caved in under the weight of a tractor.'

At night we played games, ludo or snakes and ladders, and going to bed I was given a big feed. After a couple of nights I observed my cousins drinking a fizzy drink.

'What's that you're drinking, John?'

'It's good for you, boy. Would you like some?'

'Ay.'

Filling a blue enamel mug with water he put some powder in and stirred it around.

'Here, drink it before the fizzing stops. It's nice though a wee bit salty. Mammy says it's good for your insides, but only drink it when you're going to bed.'

That evening when no one was about I sneaked into the kitchen several times and found the blue and white tin. Feeling bloated, I could drink no more and went to bed. In the early hours of the morning I was attacked by cramps so unbearable I had to wake my cousin.

'Hold on, John, through here,' he said.

He led me to the outside toilet and I sat there for an hour moaning and clutching my stomach.

'What have you been at, boy?' he asked eventually.

'That fizzy drink that's good for your insides.'

He explained that it was 'Andrews Liver Salts' but I still did not understand.

'Jaysus, haven't you had a laxative before?'

'Laxative?'

'Yes, laxative, mammy swears by it.'

'Well, maybe she does but I'm having no more of it,' I groaned.

The *Armagh Gazette* carried father's long obituary and the funeral was attended by many important people, some from as far away as County Monaghan; men from the Ministry and the Milk Marketing Board, cattle-dealers, auctioneers and all the surrounding farming community. Cars filled the yard and hayshed, others lined the lanes, causing chaos for hours.

It took us months to come to terms with the fact that we were now on our own. When I arrived home from the Hunters it was to encounter a much-changed William. Mischievousness had given way to a certain darkness. No longer did he crawl beneath my bed, raising it on his back to scare the wits out of me. He was not yet twenty-one and there was talk of the need for a legal guardian until he came of age. The Hunters took up the role but William insisted it would not be for very long, he would take over soon, and, as far as Violet and I were concerned, he was boss.

On my first day back at school, Miss Clarke surveyed me sadly. 'I'm very sorry, John. Now sit up here at the front with Ivan Greer. You and Violet must continue with the school concert.'

I was looking forward to the big day we had been rehearsing for since mother's death. The date was to coincide with leaving Miss Clarke and starting at a new school in Markethill. Half an hour before home-time, Jacky Riddle, a tall stooping lad with a rasping cough leaned over my desk and mocked, 'Ha ha, oul Willie Hughes is dead.'

I felt sick. 'I'll get you when the bell goes, Riddle.'

He had quite a start on me as we entered the pine plantation. I had not been this way before and the dark dampness of the place surprised me, slowing my steps till the trees began to thin out towards a meadow. Quickening my pace through the spongy greenness I heard his chest rattling. His long legs slowed down and at the river he tripped and fell into the water with a yell. That subdued him and he pathetically offered to take me hunting with his brother. I wanted to hit him but stormed away instead and rode home in a fury.

William was our mainstay now. Unlike father he was lean and wiry, slightly hunched, with beautiful eyes that riveted attention to his weathered hook-nosed face but never betrayed the turmoil within. Beaten many times by my father, he neither flinched nor floundered and I had seen him stand before the belt with no attempt to protect himself, fasten his gaze on my father and when the leathering was done, say, 'Have you finished now?'

Within a short space of time it was known that the new gaffer-to-be of Lisnagat was no less formidable than the old. Although not yet in full command, he changed the name on the tractor from William A. Hughes to Hughes Brothers.

A few days after the funeral the Hunters set about fulfilling their duty as official guardians. At this time there was talk of Violet and me going into an orphanage. I am sure Aunt Ruth and Uncle John did not want this but in any case it would have made no difference. William's face darkened and his threat to shoot anyone who tried it was not ignored.

'Violet and John stay with me. The oul fella would not have wanted it, and I will not have it. Anyone who tries it will have to get by me first.'

Joe expressed similar feelings and in the face of such determination, the subject was never again mentioned. I am sure the Hunters did their job with what they believed were the best interests of the family at heart. However, it caused great pain and humiliation to see our father's affairs examined in minute detail. Some debts were revealed and most of our livestock had to be sold to meet outstanding commitments. William and Joe explained that father always paid his bills on an agreed yearly basis and the debts were far outweighed by the value of assets.

'Sure it's not much, Aunt Ruth, I'll get it down,' said William confidently. 'Da traded like this for twenty years.'

'You're not starting like this, William. We'll have a clean slate,' she insisted and the Hunters had their way. Everything went except the cows. When the wagon came for our proud herd of white Hereford bullocks the hard young man faced his task. Only the ferocity with which he set about loading the wagon, and the cold brilliance of his eyes, marked the task as different. 'It will be a long time before we see a herd the likes of that again. The oul fella will haunt me,' he said.

Some years later I was to see documented evidence of the considerable value of my father's estate. It proved my brother's viewpoint. However, thirty-years ago in Ireland a small mortgage or a wee loan from the bank, which would have prevented much hardship, was shameful.

Such was the dark veil shrouding good business sense, and protecting the rigid belief that kept people in their corridors of misery.

The bitter struggle to keep the place going had begun and William and Joe worked hard, shouldering the enormous responsibility of two farms and a family. William aged noticeably, concentrating now on arable crops with the help of Uncle John Hughes. This well-liked man soon became a father-figure, always there to help and advise. He and his eldest son, John, were a light-hearted pair, finding something to laugh about, no matter what the problem.

The tractor-driving lessons I had received at Aunt Ruth's tempted me to start our machine. Driving it just a few feet forward I always left it back in exactly the same place for fear of William finding out. Cousin John Hughes was good at everything and I was desperate to learn the things he knew, feeling envious, frustrated and full of admiration.

Aunt Ruth's final act before William took over caused much embarrassment. She applied to the church for an allowance to provide school uniforms for Violet and me. Obviously they would consider only hardship cases, but yet again, this formidable woman had her way and sixty-five pounds a year was granted.

As the months went by, the pain of father's death began to ease, and now that the big night of the school concert was nigh, I felt tremendous excitement at the prospect of being important.

Seven

❧

On concert day, Miss Clarke sent us home early.

'Don't be late, John and Violet, are you getting a lift?'

'Yes, Miss.'

'Not on the tractor, I hope, you must look nice.'

'No, our Auntie is bringing us.'

At home William was busy.

'We won't be coming. There's a cow calving, and Joe's gone to Hughes's to help mend the hydraulics in the tractor. Farson's Garage would fleece a man.'

After I had polished my crinkled brown shoes, Violet knotted my tie.

'Sure there's a ring around your neck, you're not going like that,' she said with disgust. 'Take off your shirt and wash yourself proper. Quick, here she comes.'

'Let's have a look at you,' said Aunt Ruth, twisting my neck and peering into my ears. 'You'll do, come on.'

We sat in the back with Cousins John and Pearl while Betty drove, leaving Aunt Ruth to chatter all the way.

'Don't forget your lines. Don't sniffle, have you got a hanky? Here, take this comb, wee John, and do your hair before you go on.'

'Oh leave him alone, Mammy, you're like an oul turkey, he's nervous enough,' chided Betty.

We arrived at seven, our faces red and shiny with anxiety at the sight of so many folk filing into the hall. Aunt Ruth had sold dozens of tickets, telling everyone that they could not miss our singing and acting. Backstage Mrs Allen went over the song with us, making sure we could do it without the sheets. Miss Clarke quietly reassured us and reminded us not to rush. The first half of the concert was a comedy sketch in which Mervyn Baird played the part of a clown. Sitting with the audience, Violet and I curled up with laughter and forgot our nervousness. I could hardly wait to get out on stage for my turn to make them laugh. Aunt Ruth's face was gleaming out of the darkness as I cheerily recited a humorous poem called 'Thaddy Molloy'.

When I finished they laughed, cheered, and banged their form seats shouting 'Again, again.' Ivan read 'The Charge of the Light Brigade', greatly impressing us with the drama of his performance, but the climax of the show was two duets sung by Violet and me. Holding hands and gazing awkwardly into each other's eyes, we sang 'Oh no, John', then on a nod from Miss Clarke we moved to a corner of the stage, sat down by a mock church door and plaintively sang 'Two Little Orphans'.

> *Two little orphans, a boy and a girl,*
> *Sat by an old church door*
> *The little girl's feet were as black as the curls*
> *That fell on the dress that she wore.*
>
> *The boy's coat was faded and hatless his head,*
> *A tear shone in each little eye.*
> *'Why don't you go home to your mother?' I said*
> *And this was the maiden's reply.*
>
> *'Mama's in Heaven, they took her away*
> *And left Jim and I all alone.*
> *We came here to stay 'til the close of the day*
> *For we have no Mama, no home.*
>
> *We can't earn our bread, we're too little,' she said*
> *'Jim's five and I'm only seven.*
> *We've no one to love us, our Papa is dead*
> *And our darling Mama's in Heaven.*
>
> *Papa was lost out at sea long ago,*
> *We waited all night on the shore*

For he was a Life-Saving Captain you know,
But he never came back any more.

Then Mama got sick, angels took her away
They said to a home fair and bright.
She said she would come for her darlings some day,
Perhaps she is coming tonight.

Maybe tonight there's no room,' she said
'Two little ones to keep,'
And placing an arm under little Jim's head
She kissed him and both fell asleep.

The Sexton came early to ring the church bell,
He found them both covered snow white,
The angels made room for two children to dwell
In Heaven with Mammy that night.
In Heaven with Mammy tonight.

At the end I had to give Violet a kiss and the audience clapped and cheered again. Making our way down to Aunt Ruth people crowded around and patted our heads.

'Your father would've been proud,' they said.

Miss Clarke was delighted with our performance and reluctantly I said goodbye to her for the last time.

Back home Aunt Ruth excitedly told William how good we had been.

'And Jaysus, William, you should have heard wee John doing "Thaddy Molloy".'

'Well, I'm glad to hear he can do something well,' said William with a sneer.

The singing of 'Two Little Orphans' hurt me for months afterwards. I thought about it constantly and rebellious anger gripped me. Violet and I were chosen because our parents were dead. Most of all I was upset at lacking the courage to refuse to sing and to tell them that there was no heaven.

Now twenty-one, William had changed into a dour brooding man whose authority was most frequently expressed through repeated stinging cuffs to my head. I began to believe that I was indeed useless and though I tried desperately to please by digging the garden, washing out the byre, or sweeping the yard, nothing satisfied him and the cuffs gave way to beatings. I could cope with the sharp slaps and kicks on the behind from Joe when his fiery temper erupted, but William's cold anger terrified me. With father gone I felt very vulnerable.

Molly, near to school-leaving, was showing an interest in boys and her green eyes and blond hair captivated Seymour Shields.

William had known him since boyhood and trusted the handsome well-dressed young man. One Saturday he called for Molly who looked a picture in a green dress blown out by a starched petticoat.

'Your slip is showing, Molly,' teased Seymour.

'So's your father,' she flashed.

'Is William not about? Ah, there he is.'

'How's she cuttin', Billy?'

'Could be better, Seymour. I missed the milk wagon this morning by about five minutes and had to drive to Tassagh. I'll see that driver in hell yet.'

'Could you and Joe give us a hand with the threshing in two weeks' time?' Seymour asked.

'Jaysus, you're early. We'll be at least a month yet and Uncle John Hughes needs help too.'

'Have I starched this dress for nothin', Seymour Shields?' asked Molly furiously. 'I thought you were here to take me to the dance, but if you'd rather blether about threshing then don't mind me.'

'I've minded you for many an hour, Molly Hughes, but we're done now so hop in the car. I'm away, Billy, before she rares up any more.'

My sister, although growing up, was not without girlish mischievousness. The Livingstones' farm was an old grey building with scattered outhouses, the yard a slurry of mud, paddled by ducks and geese. On the way home from school Molly always bullied me into knocking on the door to ask the time or for a drink of water. Mrs Livingstone would answer, her corn-sack apron covered in flour, and her hands sticky with dough. Savouring the smells of baking and seasoned fruit, I'd quickly sip the water, then give her my expectant look.

'Would you like a few of these?' she'd ask, filling my school-bag with apples and pears.

Their farm was overrun with cats, and soon we were accepting kittens instead of fruit. They messed in our hay-shed and grain stores. William cursed us and, bundling them into sacks, dumped them on the roadside a few yards from the Livingstones' farm. Next evening I knocked as usual to enquire the time.

'It's four o'clock,' snapped Mrs Livingstone, and closed the door.

Molly now switched her attention to Johnson's orchard further along the road.

'Right, John, we'll put your books into my bag and remember, we want the red ones off the little tree.'

'I don't want to go, Molly.'

'Sure what's wrong? Are you feared or somethin'?'

'No, but Johnson might get me.'

'No he won't. Keep down as you run.'

'No. Why don't you go? You've got green eyes and greedy guts.'

'Oh go on, John, I only want to taste a few and I'll do your homework for you.'

That decided it and I ventured in, eyes fixed nervously on the windows of Johnson's house as I groped at the branches and clambered up. With my satchel full I was making my way back down when I heard him.

'I'll kick your arse, young Hughes, leave them apples! ' he raged, roaring down the orchard. My belly churning, I fell out over the hedge and ran. Still shouting, Johnson was catching up.

'I'm sorry, Mister. I won't do it again,' I yelled.

'By Jaysus, you'll be sorry if I catch a hold of you.'

There was only one thing to do. I dropped the bag and

he stopped the chase. At the top of Finlay's Hill I caught up with a giggling Molly and Violet.

'It's alright for youse two,' I blurted.

'Where's your school-bag?' laughed Molly.

'I dropped it. William'll kill me.'

'Give over, sure he's in Armagh all day. You can have mine anyway. I won't be needin' it after tomorrow.'

The next day Molly put on a new blue dress and white shoes for her last day at school. Her carefree attitude changed as always when approaching Donelly's Farm on the way home.

'Oh I hope they're not out.'

We were all scared of Donelly's goats but Molly had a notion in her head that they were after her. Violet and I tried to convince her to walk quickly by as most of the time they were busy up the banks chewing hawthorn.

'I hope he shoots Big Grey for the threshing this year,' she whispered as we crept past.

It was traditional for farmers to feed the men on best beef at harvesting time but father always believed that Donelly shot a goat for this festive gathering and not one of his smelly hedge-nibbling pets either. Up on the wilds of Clady Hills an ageing buck would meet his end and then be buried in the yard for a week to tenderize.

Goats are inquisitive creatures and Molly's nervous behaviour drew their attention. 'Oh will youse look at them, they're out, and big Grey's there as well, the smelly oul frigger. Just waitin' for me, he is,' she moaned, holding on to Violet. Big Grey turned his head, jaws motionless, before shifting his position on the bank. It was too much for Molly, and tears streamed down her face.

'Go away, go away,' she screamed.

'He's nowhere near you, Molly,' Violet stressed, urging her to move on.

As the now captivated goat trotted down the bank and across the road Molly grabbed my shoulders, and held me to her for a shield whilst Big Grey attempted to corner us. He had taken a fancy to her lovely dress with its tent-shaped skirt. Standing back in awe of Molly's hysterical shrieks, I watched him tilt his head sideways and rip her clothing to shreds with his horns. Just then Tommy Donelly came out and chased the marauder away. Piteously, Molly inspected her dress.

'They ought to be locked up,' she sniffed.

'Not at all. They're harmless enough if you ignore them,' he scoffed.

'This isn't harmless, is it?' she said, holding out her ripped dress. 'Still, there'll be one less after you've done your threshing,' she blazed. 'Which one's for the bullet this year? Shoot old Grey and you'll get Christmas out of him as well.'

'You've got a neck and a half on you, Molly Hughes,' fumed Donelly. 'If your Da could hear you he'd turn in his grave. God help the poor man that takes you to the altar.'

'Well, he won't have black teeth and smell of pig-shit, that's for sure,' retorted Molly, and wheeling around she strode haughtily on.

The goats had returned to their munching and Violet and I kicked a pebble home.

Eight

W ooden poles threaded with metal cables punctuated our skyline now, the darkly creo-soted intruders issuing an unfamiliar buzz that signalled change. Not everyone could afford to take advantage of what many called 'as near a miracle as we'll ever get'. Some of the older folk were not convinced it would work.

'Holy Jaysus! You say the place will light up if you press a switch? What will they think of next? Well, we'll hold on to our tilley-lamps just in case.'

William was enthusiastic.

'The oul fella never had a chance like this and them oul hurricane-lamps keep going out,' he said excitedly.

When Cousin John Hunter said you could buy a kettle that boiled in a couple of minutes, I laughed.

'Don't take me for an eejit, boy,' I said.

'Honest to God, John, you can make tay in no time at all.'

It took several weeks for Billy Ritchie to complete the work, knocking holes in walls, and ripping up floorboards which he left for us to put back. Most of the outhouses were given lights, one in the byre and two in the hayshed.

This would be very useful after milking when we raked hay through into the byre to feed the cows. William chuckled when the big day came to switch on.

'Do you think it'll work, Billy?' he asked.

'As sure as it will rain tomorrow,' Billy assured him.

Everyone smiled with delight as light flashed into the strip-tubes on the kitchen ceiling. Violet scurried round cleaning as the brightness searched out corners that had never seen a rag-cloth. I ran about switching on lights. Everywhere looked so much bigger. The light from the bulkhead outside cast an eerie glow over the yard, and I wondered if this was what King Solomon's Mine had looked like. William put his finger into the electric kettle to see if it was getting hot.

'Jaysus Christ, I won't do that again,' he yelped, and jumped back shaking his fingers.

'Listen to her, she's singing like a good 'un,' he said.

Tentatively we sipped the tea. 'Yes, it's good,' we all agreed.

Now I had an advantage over the rats in the byre. Creeping up to the door I could flick the switch and run down the walkway with plenty of time for a clear shot.

Aunt Ruth insisted that Violet and I continue going to church. After an hour sitting on the shiny pews in Glassdrummond parish church I became accustomed to the cold. The stone pillars and walls radiated coldness with only an occasional patch of sunlight penetrating the leaded windows to cast dusky shadows on the floor. Today, however, it was Harvest Thanksgiving and a sight to behold. Sheaves of golden corn and barley hung around the walls; baskets of apples, pears and plums stood with flowers and loaves of home-made bread and, closest to the altar, a perfectly shaped stook of corn. Canon Kerr, his robes swishing, walked up to the pulpit and a hush fell over the congregation as he thanked God for the good weather before attributing to His Good Grace the ability to bend our backs. Glancing at the sombre red-faced men I wondered what was in their minds as they sang the hymn that vexed William so much when it came to the line, 'All is safely gathered in.' At home William added his amendment – 'All is safely gathered in bar the butt.'

The butt was the base of the sheaves left standing to dry out after summer storms had flooded the land, bogging tractors and binders. My brothers had worked very hard before joining the congregation for this well-attended festivity. First came weeks of back-wrenching labour, cutting, tying and stooking corn, then a drying-out period before hutting. Sitting on the trailer-load of sheaves I felt excited as we bounced our way home. Unhitched from the tractor at the rear of the shed, it was left for Uncle John Hughes and son to build the stack while I went back with my brothers for another load. Eventually four golden stacks, standing high and wide, made everything worth while. On threshing morning the distant roar of the Fordson Major could be heard, and before long Uncle John Hunter came driving slowly down the lane, the big red thresher dipping from side to side as the wheels ran into ruts. He manoeuvred the huge machine into place between the stacks, placed the well-worn belts on the pulley, and with a few adjustments the tall gaunt-faced man was ready. Soon the yard was full of willing men, hobnailed boots scrunching the stones as they greeted each other, pitchforks over their shoulders. Many handshakes and swapping of stories with friends not seen since last year were interrupted by uncle's shouts, 'Come on now or we'll be here till Christmas.'

Years of harvesting had left this very experienced threshing man partially deaf. The habit of shouting above the noise of the machinery stayed with him as though the humming were trapped forever in his ears. Highly skilled at feeding sheaves into the machine, his forkers were chosen for their ability to pitch two sheaves accurately in position by his side in time with his loading rhythm. Joe was an excellent forker with endless stamina. Sackers had to leave sufficient material at the neck of the sacks for them to be gripped. Men on the baling at the opposite end to the sackers had an itchy job. Straw, an important by-product for the bedding and feeding of cattle, came tumbling down from three wooden scoops in an endless stream, with chaff and debris. Binder twine, used to secure the bales, left hands covered in welts as the straw was heaved onto trailers for stacking in the shed. Money seldom changed hands on these occasions; it was community labour, with everyone helping everyone till all the harvest was in. At about this time we saw a gradual infiltration of combine harvesters, and it saddened me to see majestic old threshers standing idle gathering grass and briars, the wooden scoops gaping like open mouths.

Feeding twenty for three days during threshing kept Mrs Goodfellow and Molly busy. The machine never stopped but hungry men filed into the kitchen to be fed in shifts on ham or corned beef and Mrs Goodfellow's renowned soda farls and slim bread. Tables and chairs were crammed tightly together leaving just enough room for the two women to squeeze by, offering long or short tea. Long tea, their way of amusing themselves, was poured from a height of two feet or so. There were not many takers.

Ratting was an important and exciting event during the harvest. A bale surround enclosing the stacks provided a ring for the men to show their dogs. Most were terriers with a fast turn but Spot was the envy of all. With head cocked to one side, one ear up, his nose twitched as the stack was reduced to a foot high. When terrified rats broke cover, the cry went up and dogs scurried criss-cross, snip-snapping, white bellies flashing. If one or two broke through the gauntlet the children chased with flailing sticks to halt the escape to the ditch.

After a hard day's threshing, my brothers, helped by Vincent Carlisle, tackled the evening milking. Vincent, employed on a casual basis for such seasonable tasks as hedge-laying, potato-lifting, and harvesting, scorned the Alpha Lavall milking machines father had installed, preferring to hand-milk. All our family loved Vincent with his red moon face and straw-blond hair peeping out from under his cap.

After the last weary men departed, Vincent helped me wash the cows' udders and tie their tails together to prevent a stinging whip across the face.

'You won't be seeing much more of me after next week, William,' he said.

'Why? Surely you're not off to Australia again are you?'

'I am, I'm tellin' you. I mean it this time.'

'Stop giving out, Vincent, it's only your mind will go.'

'Just you wait and see, and I'll have you know, Billy Hughes, they've got machines out there to cut hedges. I'm tellin' youse all I need's a reference and I'll be away with myself.'

'Well, give me a pen and I'll do one for you now.'

'Sure there's no rush, Billy, it'll do next time I see you.'

'Have you seen "himself" lately?' Vincent asked, to change the subject. 'Wouldn't you think of giving him the start, Billy? Jaysus, with a back like that he'd tie a brave oul louch of corn.'

'Kiss my arse, Vincy, one eejit round here's enough,' said William derisively.

Our best yield of corn was off land rented from 'himself', a man thought by most to be away in the head. Joe, a skilled negotiator, struck the deal where others had failed. Perhaps in England the men in white coats would have ended his freedom, but in Ireland, he was looked upon as harmless enough.

'Holy Jaysus, will youse look at yer man, he's got somethin' wrong that's not right,' the locals would say.

Harold Anderson's old farmhouse with its quiet winding lane sat in a hollow a mile away from us. Glorious orchards surrounded the lonely dark house, and the wild rambling trees were left unattended. Cousin John Hughes and I gorged ourselves on fallen fruit before it rotted back into the sodden earth. Harold's dead father had been head-master at Clady School during the 'forties, and he instilled in his son the importance of reading. Harold's love of riding took him out most days and often he could be seen charging along the grass verges without saddle or reins.

The B Specials were now becoming more in evidence and twice a week patrolled main crossroads. Harold took exception to the fact that the roads crossing near his lane did not warrant their attention, and decided to do the job himself. Stopped by a 'Halt! Who goes there?' William would impatiently wind down the window, announcing, 'Hughes brothers, Harold.'

'Hold your horses, Billy Hughes,' Harold would reply and, turning round, command the same of another motorist coming from the other direction, then, with a wave of his enormous craggy hand, wave us on.

'About bloody time,' William would mutter, but he never forgot to raise his hand in salute.

There were those amongst the locals who thought they could get the better of Harold when he had a heifer going cheap. Many a night's milking was late because one or other of the Donelly brothers called at Harold's house. One evening a broad strong face appeared at the door and a thick hairy arm guided one of the Donellys in. Then, snapping over the bolts, Harold put the key in his pocket. Motioning the nervous man to sit down, Harold disappeared for a few minutes, to reappear with a mug of goat's milk and a book. After forcing down the milk, the bargain-hunter was given the book and told to read. 'Himself' sat reading opposite, occasionally giving his captive a stern glance. At about ten o'clock, after a thorough quizzing on the few pages poor Donelly had managed to read, Harold let him leave with never a mention of a heifer.

Uncle John Hughes recalled the time when some poor man, curious to see if Harold had any livestock, went snooping around his orchards. Leaping out from behind a bush Harold caught hold of the intruder's coat-collar and marched him into the house, where he sat him down and ordered him to recite the last verse of the Lord's Prayer. The terrified man did not even know the first but he did when he left, and Uncle John swore he could be heard muttering 'Thy kingdom come' for years afterwards.

Nine

The Hunters relinquished their position as our legal guardians, and William was finally in command. However, the Church clothing allowance was still paid to Aunt Ruth, so during the summer holidays of 1960 she marched Violet and me into Morgan's draper's shop one Saturday afternoon to get us rigged out for the new Markethill Secondary Intermediate School.

My excitement at receiving new clothes was marred when the old draper came out from behind the counter with shorts and plimsolls.

'And they'll need cream to clean the gutties with. I've heard the PT master is very strict and likes the childer to look smart, especially at school games,' he said.

'I don't want to do games, Aunt Ruth,' I complained.

'Give over, will you, of course you do, it will make a man out of you,' she responded briskly.

I knew I was fine at running down Seaboughan Lane to fetch home the cows, and sure-footed over ruts and tufts of grass when flying along the headland on corn-cutting days, but the thought of organized games filled my belly with butterflies.

The draper nudged an assistant, 'Parcel up those uniforms for Mrs Hunter, I'll have a count-up.'

'Jaysus, it can't be that long,' fired Aunt Ruth, watching him closely. 'If our Betty was here she'd have done it in her head long ago.'

'Maybe she would but I'm not getting any younger these days.'

The scribbling on the shoe-box stopped and was re-placed by intense mutterings, interspersed with soft whis-tles through the gaps in his teeth.

'Right, Mrs Hunter, that'll be thirty-nine pounds, two and sixpence.'

'Ah Jaysus, surely to God you're not going to charge me that for two little orphans, are you?'

'I've got a living to make, Missus, we'll call it thirty-seven.'

'Couldn't you see your way to calling it thirty-five?'

'Look, thirty-six, and I'm doing myself.'

'Ah Jaysus, you're a lovely man. Someone'll see you in heaven. I'll dance at your wedding, drink at your wake, and cry at your funeral.'

We made for the door laden with brown-paper parcels and the draper wished Violet and me 'health to wear'. Aunt Ruth shook his hand telling him once again what a lovely man he was.

'Just a wee moment, Mrs Hunter, there's something I almost forgot,' he said, nipping across the floor to the yew-coloured cabinet.

'He'll need two pairs of these.'

'Jaysus, you'll have me selling my hens before we're finished,' she grumbled.

She paid for the underpants and, back in the car, warned us to look after the clothes.

'Hang them up after school, do you hear me now? You'll have me skint, half the allowance is gone already.'

Unlike us, our cousins took readily to change, and were enthusiastic about the opening of the new school, probably because they were safely outside the catchment area. Their continuous talk made me jittery. Betty raved about the gymnasium.

'Youse'll be fit, I can tell you that. They have a buck, a horse, wall-bars, a medicine ball, and a whole clatter of apparatus, and you'll have assembly every morning.'

'What's that for?' I asked.

'To sing and say prayers.'

'But I do that on Sundays.'

'Maybe you do but I'll warn you, John, it's not Cladymore you're going to now. No dawdling along the road. The cane comes out if you're late for roll-call.'

'Roll-call?'

'Aye, your name's shouted out each morning and Kelly the science master stands no nonsense.'

'Sure, what good's science going to do for me?'

'It's a great chance for you to become educated, John. You'll be lighting bunsen burners and doing experiments. I've done it myself, you never know when it'll come in useful.'

'You'll do metalwork and woodwork, and there's a teacher for every subject, and they send out a report on you each year,' Cousin John informed me.

The revelation of a school report really worried me. My lack of interest in learning would be exposed and this meant only one thing – trouble with William.

'Watch out for Terry Soullier, boy, he's a French-Canadian and a real hard case, you can't miss him. Jet-black hair and very good-looking,' warned John.

On the first day, feeling awkward in my crisp uniform, I cycled off in dread with Violet. Parking our bicycles in the covered shed we mingled with the few pupils we knew. I looked around nervously for Terry Soullier. Surely that must be him, I thought, as I saw a gum-chewing lad with an uncanny resemblance to Elvis Presley. Already he was holding court with two girls and combing his black waves. A stocky master came out.

'Right. Line up in single file and walk into assembly.'

'That's Webster,' someone muttered.

In the assembly hall the buzz of voices was drowned by Kelly's thunderous tones. 'Quiet, all of you. Welcome to Markethill Secondary Intermediate. We will commence assembly with a hymn.'

After singing 'We plough the fields and scatter' I reluctantly joined the others in the Lord's Prayer, and my mind flashed back to Harold Anderson. Gazing around, I noticed the wall-bars that stretched all along one side.

'You have to climb them like a monkey,' came a whisper from behind.

Turning round, my eyes locked onto Soullier. 'What are you lookin' at?'

His arrogant voice startled me, then Violet nudged me. 'It's you. Say "present sir".'

'Present,' my voice squeaked. Kelly roared.

'Hughes. Say "present sir" clearly. You're either here or you're not here, and if you are here let me know you're here.'

After roll-call the headmaster told us the rules. Holding a cane in one hand he slowly tapped the other palm. I could see dandruff on his collar, and occasionally he raked back a lank piece of hair. Rocking on his heels he surveyed the hall.

'And finally I would say, I don't like caning pupils, but I will if I have to.'

After school most youngsters went around the town or idled along the disused railway embankment but I rushed home to meet Shep at the end of the lane.

When he went missing one evening, my brothers and sisters seemed unconcerned by my shouts as I raced around calling him.

'Sure he might have run off somewhere, John,' Molly suggested.

Scouring Seaboughan Lane, I raced over the river and way beyond into the top fields. The shirt stuck to my back and panic gripped me. Shep loved me, he would never run off; where was he? On my return Molly was waiting in the back yard.

'I can't find him, Molly, something's wrong.'

'Will you come now and have your pie, John?'

'No, I'm going for Patsy to help me.'

Molly wrung her hands and spoke in a hesitant voice.

'John, Shep is dead. William had to shoot him, he's been killing sheep.'

'He wouldn't, he wouldn't,' I yelled.

'He did. William found him with Clarke's Jack Russell.'

'Well, it must have been him then that done the killing. Shep's a sheepdog,' I shouted.

'John, there was blood on his mouth.'

Leading me through the old kitchen, she sat me down by the table.

'Here now, cut your crying and you can have my apple pie as well.'

'I don't want any. How did he shoot him?' I asked chokingly. She did not reply.

'Tell me, will you, Molly.'

Reluctantly she explained. 'William didn't get close enough and Shep ran off wounded, but Jackie Love came with his long gun and managed to track him down. This time there was no mistake.'

When William came home he said, 'It couldn't be helped. He's been killing sheep, running with Clarke's Jack Russell. He's been shot as well.'

We spoke no more. Later that night I asked Joe to show me where Shep was buried. Leading me past the flax-hole, he stopped at a stinking old shuck where brambles and briars had been battered down.

'I buried him there.'

The yellow clay oozed water and I could see the marks where the shovel had beaten it down.

'That's enough of crying now,' he said and left me.

After putting some big stones on the grave I pressed a penny deep into the clay and cried. Black birds twittered and a crimson sun edged over Seaboughan Hill. A moorhen croaked as I lobbed a stone into the flax-hole. Back in the kitchen no one spoke and I went to bed. The next evening when I saw Patsy it was as if he knew. Forlorn and narrow-eyed, he listened.

'Could he not have been tied up?'

I shrugged my shoulders.

'I'm sorry for you, boy, honest to God I am, I know what's in your head.'

Years before, their black and white collie had died from gunshot wounds. I don't think my father had meant to hurt him, just frighten him off from stealing our eggs out of the outlying nests. When we sat in the damp shade of the orchard I remembered the day well. The Goodfellow family, gathered by the top field gate, must have seen father standing in the hedge with his gun because they called their old dog frantically, but as he lumbered towards them father fired.

It took a long time to accept Shep's death and to this day I remember the beautiful dog my father bought me. I also remain convinced he knew he was dying and Shep was a farewell gift, my companion for the future. From as far back as I can recall, dogs were an important part of my life and in the same year that Shep died I saw an opportunity to have another friend. One scorching Saturday afternoon, I noticed something lying at the bottom of the field that ran parallel with Seaboughan Lane. Approaching hesitantly I could see that it was a dog. Whining pitifully, it made no attempt to stand. As I knelt down the tail began to move slowly and I reached out to touch it, but before I had a chance to pull back, its teeth sank deep into my arm. Jumping up with blood pouring from the holes I ran up the field to find William.

'That'll larn ya for sticking your neb in where it's not wanted,' was all he said.

My arm by now was dripping and I could not believe that he was refusing to take me to the doctor in Markethill. Washing the blood off under the scullery tap I held a rag-cloth against the wound. When the bleeding stopped, two distinct holes could be seen turning a bluish-black colour, and I could see into where the skin lay puckered. The ride to Markethill was tricky and when my arm started to bleed again I held it against my chest thinking of the swanky town kids who were able to ride with no hands at all.

The surgery was closed, but after a lot of banging the doctor's irritated face appeared at the door.

'I've burst my arm, look, there's holes in it,' I blurted out tearfully.

'Come in here and sit down. What bit you?' he asked.

'An oul dog.'

After a close look he gave me an injection which he said would stop lockjaw and then dabbed the wound with iodine.

'Here's another bandage. Get your sister to wash and change it every few days. Now tell me, where's the dog now?'

'Ach, sure me brother will've done away with 'im.'

'Best thing to do if he's turning to biting people, now push your bike home, and no pressure on that arm for a few weeks.'

I went to bed that night in despair. All my family seemed to accept that William was justified in taking a shot at the dog seen crossing our fields in the early morning. I couldn't work out to this day why the poor creature was left to die a lingering death. I lay there thinking about how the Hunters had forced Violet and me to join the Orange Order even though we hated it. On a local march through Mount Norris village, I had beaten my triangle so hard and fast it rang in my ears for a week. Uncle John had halted the march, silenced his lambeg drum and ordered me back to the hall. I never paraded again.

At about three o'clock in the morning I began to drift in and out of a dream-haunted sleep.

I felt sick with sadness. My best friend Patsy Goodfellow was dead. He lay on the slope of a dark hill, his green tunic torn, blood swamping his chest and trickling from his mouth. He looked forlorn in death, his long legs raised at an angle, suggesting he had made a gallant attempt to stand up and fight. It was 13 July. I was at Scarva where annually they reenact the Battle of the Boyne and I trod up the slope to survey the carnage.

Dreaming or not, the incident affected me badly. Here was the friend I cherished, dead, and I was part of it.

Ten

❧

Television would never catch on as far as country people were concerned. We had all heard of the small screen you could have in the house but only good-for-nothing loafers who weren't prepared to do a hand's turn about the place would have anything to do with it.

Our pastimes reflected the skills and customs of country life. Stone-skimming across the disused flax-hole was restricted because years of accumulated debris had considerably shortened its length. Flax harvesting had long since been abandoned because it was hard and sometimes dangerous work producing the fibre for this fine linen. Both my brothers were expert stone-skimmers and William taught me the art.

'Get yourself a flat stone, Lippy. Crouch down more and get in line with the water's level. Look, like this.'

I watched him practise the swing, bringing his arm around to his side before unleashing his coiled muscles. The stone bounced seven times.

'There you are, how's that? Come on, have a crack at it yourself. Well, four isn't bad; keep at it, you can win coppers if you're really good.'

Beside the deep litter house William placed bottles and cans on a jagged stone wall and took on all comers, throwing freehand or shooting his favourite catapult made of blackthorn and bicycle tubing. He could stun a rabbit at twenty yards or knock a jackdaw off a chimney. I couldn't even draw back his ash-bows and would watch wide-eyed as his arrows thudded into turnips at a distance my old air-rifle could just about manage.

My favourite game was pitch-and-toss because it gave me the chance to win money. If it was raining we played in the warmth of the byre and when the sun was out a well-swept patch in our yard might be the pitching place, but the most popular spot was the crossroads by the Gospel Hall, a short distance from our house. This had the added advantage of enticing George, Fran and Patsy Goodfellow along from their cottage only two hundred yards away. With Gougho, Vincent Carlisle, Bob McClure, my brothers and I, nine players meant a fat pot. A gravelled road is not an easy pitching ground because rough surfaces tend to inhibit the slide of the coin. Normally the pitch commenced with coppers, moving up to threepenny bits, tanners and shillings as the game gathered momentum.

Whoever pitched their coin nearest the stone tossed first, the next closest taking their turn, ending with the one farthest away. Standards of pitching were high, and with the opportunity of winning a capful of money the game could become very serious, sometimes lasting for hours. It was quite in order to re-enter or knock a winning coin out of the way provided you had the money to keep trying. This usually resulted in the elimination of Patsy and me through lack of funds. If there was little to separate the first three coins then these experts increased the stake by pitching two-shilling pieces or half-crowns till eventually a halt was reached. Outlying coins, well away from the mark, were placed in the cap.

'What fuckin' bastard has slipped de Valera in here?' asked hawk-eyed William during one heated game. 'It was you, Gougho, wasn't it? You can't be watched.'

'Not at all. Sure I haven't been to Castleblaney in months,' said Gougho, jingling the Irish shillings hidden in his pocket.

I became quite skilled at the pitching part of the game but always nominated William to toss for me. Gougho and the others did not like this, knowing that if they were lying fourth out of nine they may as well go home. He kept a close eye on William, rushing to where the coins dropped, hopeful of finding tails.

'Holy Jaysus Christ Almighty! sure leave the rest of us somethin' to toss, William, will you?' he'd plead, as time after time they came down heads.

'Get out of the way, you gabby brat,' he'd mutter when I shouted encouragement to my hero.

William, having found his rhythm, would start on the silver. Unlike the coppers which he tossed with a murderous fury, two-shilling pieces and half-crowns were placed gently on the fingers and his red sinewy arm flicked the coins up and away into a shimmering arc.

'They're ours, Lippy,' he'd roar triumphantly.

Then, with the toss finished, we'd dive home to tackle the well-overdue milking, laughing as the lads called after us. 'We'll have you robbin' hures next week.'

William, Joe and the Love brothers took me dolahan gaffing one night. Joey Love was a huge man with hands like shovels, his sausage-shaped fingers hardened with callouses. For all his cumbersome bulk he was graceful and had a ready smile. No matter the hour or request, this obliging giant never refused us help.

His elder brother Jacky, boss of their smallholding, wore a look of serious intent that broke into a satisfied grin when he conquered temperamental machinery. Everyone liked and respected the small man with grey curling hair. If William could not mend our Albion binder the solution was simple: 'I'm just going to run over to see Jacky,' he'd say.

Father used to enjoy ceilíing there to listen to the crack between opposites. If the mood in the small firelit cottage was quiet he was not beyond stirring it, and on one occasion caused a fierce row by provoking an argument about the profitability of sheep.

Joey, losing the debate, jumped off his chair and threatened, 'I'll tell you how it is, Jacky, if you don't shut your fuckin' mouth I'll throw you out in the back field with them woolly bastards of yours.'

He always said Jacky should have been a schoolteacher and Violet often took her sums to him. He solved them all in pencil, then rubbed out the answers when she assured him she understood. How they made a living was a mystery and the townland laughed when Jacky turned his front room into a shop selling drapery goods. Soon the wisdom of his venture was proven as men, rushing to get out on Saturday night to the dance, called to buy shirts and pullovers. I was sent to knock on his door many times.

'Gougho wants a pair of socks, Jacky, and William a shirt, but he says not as tight as the last one cos it's chokin' his neck.'

'How about this nice pink one, surely he'll click with that on. There you are now and tell William I said courtin' men don't need their collars done up!'

We knew Jacky was a good shot but were unaware of his expertise at gaffing.

I watched as the men removed the shafts from yard brushes and Jacky fixed sinister-looking metal hooks to the ends.

'Now watch yourselves with these, lads,' he warned as he filed them to a thin point, wrapped them in corn sacks and hid them in the back of the car with the flashlights.

'Brave night for it, men. Brave night indeed,' Jacky enthused. 'That's the glen, over the other side of that field.'

'We'll pull in here then, Jacky,' suggested William.

'Jaysus no, the police will see the car.'

Parking behind the hedge in a field well away from the river, we set off across the grass while I chattered with excitement.

'Shut up gabbing, Lippy,' said William. 'The whole frigging country will hear you.'

Down at the river's edge I could hardly contain myself as the flashlights scanned and probed the black water.

'Here's some,' I yelled.

'Will you keep your voice down, they'll be away with the noise,' snarled an anxious Jacky.

My brothers had had basic instruction in the car from

this wizard of the water.

'Now listen, men, lower your gaff slowly and gently a few feet away from the fish, then slide it under his belly and don't try to pull him out till you're right under him. Keep the flashlights on his head and try to get one on his own so as not to frighten the others away. And none of your blether either, they can hear a midge land on a leaf a mile away.'

All the rules were broken. Cries of, 'Will youse look at the size of the hures, they're built like sharks,' echoed round the chill of the glen. My job was to hit them on the head with a mallet. It was difficult to get to them all as fish flew everywhere. Some slithered down the green stones back into the water. I couldn't believe it, I had almost a sackful. The exhilaration was quelled when Joe hissed, 'Jacky, there's torches in the field.'

I looked up to see lights bouncing towards us.

'Police. Stay where you are. We're police. Stay where you are.' We gathered our belongings, slipping and sliding over the steep embankments.

'I will in my arse stay,' hissed William. 'Give me the sack, boy, and put that torch out.'

'William, my wellie's coming off,' I gasped.

'Jaysus Christ, come here will you,' and he lugged it back on.

The policemen were still shouting, 'Drop the torches, stay where you are.'

'You can kiss my arse,' laughed Joey.

'Get down and stay here,' Jacky whispered as we approached the road. 'I'll just have a look first in case they've got a man planted.'

Crawling along the hedge he peered through the thorns. 'Come on, we're away. By Jaysus, I feel like a youngster again,' laughed Joey, clearly pleased with the results.

'Can Patsy come next time, William?' I asked.

'Oh we'll have to see about that, won't we, Jacky?'

Back home we divided the catch and went to bed looking forward to a big feed the following day.

Patsy Goodfellow and I grew up together and were almost inseparable. After school I would stand at the well-trodden gap in the orchard hedge, separating our land from Marshall's big field, waiting for him to appear and sidle stiff-shouldered down towards me, his lanky athletic legs striding effortlessly. His father, a demon card-player, had a soft spot for me but he rared up if his son came home with torn clothes. A chronic chest condition prevented him from working, so money was scarce indeed. In spite of his illness, Francy Goodfellow transformed the small piece of barren land in front of their cottage into a rich vegetable plot. His potatoes were the most impressive, a rush of dark green foliage with white-flowered tops. I never saw him treat his much-needed crop against the dreaded blight. Our potato fields turned a speckled thrush-egg blue from the effects of bluestone and soda-mix spray.

Apart from mending his family's footwear Francy killed and plucked fowl for the locals to supplement his meagre income.

Patsy and I, wanting to be useful, took it upon ourselves to destroy magpies' nests. I spotted while he cleared. He cursed me if I sent him to a 'dead' nest because it was a prickly task, thorns ripping at his face and clothes. But I was usually right; the fullness of the domed shape and the new look of clay and sticks were give-away signs.

Patsy was undaunted and could penetrate the thickest of thorn bushes. Back home his father would shake his black beret at me and say, 'John Hughes, you should not be takin' our fella out with you robbin' those bloody nests. These are the only school things he has, and look at the state of them. There's more darnin' holes in that jersey than there is sheep in your fields, and by Jaysus if 'is trousers get any worse they'll be thinkin' he's Fitzpatrick 'imself.'

Fitzpatrick lived nearby on the brow of a windswept hill in a tiny, almost derelict cottage with corn sacks across the side and back windows to shelter him from the cruel elements. This small ragged man with a bushy grey moustache walked the seven miles to Armagh each day to search for cigarette ends. He was never seen without his wrinkled hat, blackened by years of sweat, and wore a shoe on the left foot, and a boot on the right, tied on with binder twine, visible under baggy trousers which barely covered his ankles. Mrs Goodfellow was terrified of him, swearing that the boot hid a cloven foot. When he walked to Markethill for his assistance money he carried a corn sack full of empty porter bottles tied to a blackthorn stick cast over his shoulder. His other stick was used to brandish at passers-by or bang on tractor bonnets and garden gates. On the inward journey he might be quiet but after a rake of porter in the town he became a howling tyrant.

'The wrath of God will fall upon all of youse. You're all sinners. Pillars of stone you'll be, mark my word. Vengeance is mine, come and confess before it's too late and I don't give a shite for any of youse. Shove your oul job up your arse, no good'll come of youse. I can tie corn with the best man here. Fuck the long and short of youse, you swanking bastards, you're nothin' but a lazy bunch of good-for-nothin' heathens. I've worked better men than youse into the ground. I'm telling you, the Lord'll come an' judge us all.'

If I saw him on the way home from school, I hung back until he passed our lonen.

One afternoon I allowed myself to be coerced into a peek at his cottage. Patsy was eager but I was frightened and stopped several times, grinding the white gravel into the black of the freshly tarred road with the toe of my dirty grey guttie.

'Come on, you,' jeered Patsy. 'You're yellow.'

'I'm not, but if he catches us … '

'I thought you said you'd be as good a man as your Da.'

'I will, I will, but I'm not as big as Da was yet. You won't leave me, will you?'

'On me mammy's deathbed, cross me heart I won't leave you.'

Nervously I walked up Lisnagat Hill until the cottage appeared.

'Patsy, there's smoke coming out of the chimney.'

'It's alright, he always has the fire going.'

'Not in the middle of summer, you eejit.'

'He does, I'm tellin' you, sure he's got no blankets.'

'How do you know?'

'Me and Benny Carlisle looked once.'

'Here,' said Patsy, 'I'll lift you up.'

He was giggling as I pulled back the sack that covered the window frame.

'Jaysus Christ,' I whispered, my heart thumping.

Smoke obscured most of the room, which was littered with porter bottles. There was no table, just a milking stool by an onion box with a plate on top. A black bucket bubbled over an open grate and the stench of cabbage filled my nostrils. Beneath a tiny barred window a sack bulging with turnips was propped precariously against an ancient tin bath.

'It's not as good as our byre. There's a trailor-load of turnips here. Patsy, he's a robbin' oul hure!'

In the right-hand corner I saw a pile of straw surrounded by piled ashes like the drills for potatoes. There was a grey gabardine coat in the middle with a blackened hat at the top. It was just dawning on me that he was never without his hat when the rumpled garment moved.

'Holy Christ,' I shouted, and Patsy dropped me. I could hear Fitzpatrick roaring as I picked myself up. Patsy was gone.

'Can't a decent man be left in peace? I know you, I know you, let me catch a hold of you, you little skittery-arsed hure.'

In the distance I could see Patsy running like a frightened hare, his long black jacket slapping against his elbows.

'Wait, Patsy, wait for me. Yer mammy's deathbed my arse,' I yelled.

'You'll turn to salt the pair of you. Wait till you meet your maker. I'll get you, I will, youse oul bastards,' screamed Fitzpatrick.

By the age of fourteen Patsy had a powerful strength and

a courageous heart. A wry smile appeared on his craggy face as men ten years his senior tested his strength in horseplay.

Sometimes these games got a little out of hand when the older men discovered how much power he possessed, and word soon got around that Slithery Pat, as William called him, having put many a grown man down with a single punch, was not to be taken lightly. The gentle lad I had grown up with now clearly sensed the oppression that existed in rural Ireland and issued a chilling warning. For my part, Patsy demonstrated his ability to survive while I became more and more frustrated with my own physical weakness.

Once or twice I saw him glare defiantly at William when he saw him hitting me, but he seemed to enjoy my brother's company when he was in a good mood.

I slowly accepted that William was right and I was, as he often said, no good to man or beast, especially as I seemed to bring trouble to a family already under pressure to keep things going.

If we had run out of pellets for the air-gun or could think of nothing else to do, Patsy and I enjoyed visiting and staying out late. I knew the difference between right and wrong but enjoyed our late-night visits to Johnny Dougan's cottage on the hump of a hill near the village of Mowhan. It meant more trouble with William when I eventually arrived home but I accepted that I was doing wrong and would be punished. Punishment was part of the daily routine now, so what difference did it make.

Johnny suffered from terrible aches and pains but still managed to tend his tiny garden where a tangle of flowers clambered over the walls and across the windows, culminating in a froth of honeysuckle around the stone archway to his front door. He would be delighted if we arrived early.

'Ah sure you're the very men I was after thinkin' of,' he'd say, limping towards us. 'Dig that wee bit for me, will youse, good lads?'

'Is your leg sore again, Johnny?' we'd ask and he'd mutter, 'Sure you know nothin' about it.'

A tilley-lamp, its shade riddled with blow holes and the fire struggling beneath wet clogged coals provided the only light as we sat talking and trying to copy the old man's habit of spitting through his front teeth. As our saliva sizzled on the damp fire we listened to his predictions for a poor harvest.

'By Jaysus, they've had it this year, mark my words, it's gonna teem all summer, most of the crops between here and Glenanne are down.'

I enjoyed these visits, which gave me the opportunity to act like a man, but talking with an unlit Players dog-end in my mouth proved difficult. Chewing the end I soon learnt to spit the tobacco out through almost closed lips and felt grown up nodding in manly agreement with his remarks. At around ten o'clock we supped from mugs filled with rich brown tea, stewed to a soupy liquor that left a bitter metallic taste lingering for hours. But we forced it down lest we appeared ungrateful and were not invited back.

'Right, I'll see you next Thursday, lads,' he'd say eventually.

'Oh we're not so sure about that, Johnny, we're very busy at the moment. I think we're looking at cattle and there's manure-spreading as well.'

Smiling, he'd reply, 'Sure I know rightly enough, whenever youse can, lads.'

After bidding him goodnight we'd cycle home feeling like real men. I knew now that I would never become a farmer. Getting away would not be easy but I must if I were ever to do anything, of that I was certain. I daydreamed about independence but still told no one, not even Patsy.

It was admiration for Johnny's flowers that awakened my interest in gardening. The walkways surrounding our house were overgrown with weeds and strewn with discarded cans and bottles. After collecting and disposing of the debris I pulled out the weeds, swept the pathways and dug a border around the triangular piece of grass at the gable side of the house. When I dug cow manure into the rosebeds, my roses flourished and my enthusiasm soared.

I tried to grow potatoes next, using small rejects because there were no seeds. William seemed pleased. With delight I watched as the potato stalks grew and grew. Eventually I could wait no longer and decided to pull one up to check. It came out easily to reveal a clamp of tiny white potatoes no bigger than marbles. I was very upset.

'They might have died of blight anyway,' said William, and a couple of weeks later they did. So I decided to return to flower gardening to brighten the gable wall. Patsy became interested too but was at a loss as to how we could acquire the plants we needed.

'That's no problem,' I assured him. 'Miss Clarke's garden at Cladymore School has a rake of them. She won't miss a few.'

'Go away with yourself,' said Patsy, shaking his head.

'Well, just come and keep a watch on,' I said.

Miss Clarke's garden was beautiful if a little eerie, as the moonlight cast creeping shadows across the grass. In spite of the comforting thought of Patsy in the hedge I rushed about nervously. The turf soaked my ankles and the memory of riding on William's back through the early mists of morning on his illicit plundering of Anderson's orchard flashed through my mind. Hot with urgency I yanked out two lupins, the size of the roots surprising me as I pushed them into a sack along with some yellow flowers. The garden seemed to have changed, shrubs looked bigger and I could not see their edges. I wondered where the wall-flowers were.

'Get down, boy, get down,' Patsy whispered as car lights flashed against a tree, momentarily freezing it in a haze of frosty grey. The car slowed a little and my neck stiffened, then eased as it picked up speed and headed off towards Crossmaglen. I found the wallflowers and helped myself to half a sackful then, bending low with a sack in each hand. I crept out to see Patsy's white face peering through the crossbars of the bikes hidden in the ditch.

'Jaysus, boy, I thought that was William, come on, he'll be out for you,' he whispered.

We tied the sacks to our crossbars and set off, riding a wobbly path. On the way we passed the school cook's home, a neat little red-roofed bungalow at the top of an embankment plastered with pansies, crimson and yellow.

'What have you come off for, boy?' asked Patsy.

'Shush, will you.'

Laying my bicycle in the ditch I crawled up the grassy bank. The damp chill of the summer night had soaked the earth, making it easy to dig deep with my hands. Patsy's face was fraught.

'By Christ, you've got some neck on you, John Hughes.'

Back at Patsy's we split the spoils.

'When are you puttin' them in, boy?'

'Tomorrow, Patsy.'

Next day I barrowed soil from my potato patch to the gable wall and with a garden trowel I had made at metal-work class I placed the roots gently into the soil. The lupins were tricky, they would have to go in the rose garden where the soil was deeper. Everyone admired them and asked where they had come from. Patsy and I said that we had found them at the far end of McCune's Lane – just growing there.

A few days later the pansies at the side of Patsy's cottage were spotted by the school cook's husband scouring the lanes on his small green motorbike for the plunderers of his wife's pride and joy. The Hunters were informed and told William.

When the tractor came to an abrupt halt in the yard, William's face was like frozen stone and fearfully I started to move away.

'Lippy, come 'ere you oul bastard. Found them, my arse, you just can't behave yourself, can you?'

By now I had learned to cover the back of my head as I cowered away. I felt dizzy after his ferocious beating but took it this time without backchat because I knew I was a thief. After the hiding, he roared, 'Now get each one of them flowers up and into a sack. I'll tek them to school. You've shamed me. The oul fella always said you were a good-for-nothing wastrel.'

Some weeks later I saw Aunt Ruth.

'Jaysus Christ, wee John, what came into your head anyway, sure I'll give you flowers and stay away from that Patsy Goodfellow. He's a bad one, I'm telling you, no good'll come of him,' she said with a worried frown.

My cousin Pearl took me to one side and said that if I ever felt like stealing anything again I should tell Aunt Ruth and she would buy it for me. I felt ashamed knowing that I was not only useless but a thief as well.

One day I overheard William telling Uncle John Hughes what had happened. Noisily I scuffled into the byre.

'Button your wallets, men, here comes the gardening thief in our midst,' he mocked.

The lupins from Miss Clarke's garden were overlooked in the handing over of the stolen flowers. In among the roses, they flourished and became William's favourites.

Eleven

🙰

Uncle Joe Hughes's return visits to Armagh set others on the road to Coventry in search of a better life.

'Sure a man can earn a fortune over there, William,' he promised. 'They're looking for good strong men, not afraid to work. I'm in a factory myself but if you want to go on the buildings you can earn a suitcase full of money.'

Certainly he seemed affluent and happy with five-pound notes in every pocket.

'Get out of here and come back with me, sure you're killing yourselves,' he advised. 'Look at your father, only forty-eight. I wanted him to come with me.'

'Well, I dunno. The oul fella stuck it so I'll do the same,' said William, and sang, 'If you ever go across the sea to Ireland, Sure if only at the closing of the day'.

A few months later George Goodfellow took the boat, followed shortly by his brother Fran. Mrs Goodfellow missed George for his quiet unassuming nature and ability to keep the younger children in check. I missed Fran for his humour and mimicry. A prankster and keen gambler, he often played pitch-and-toss with William in the yard until dusk.

My brothers showed no concern when Gougho lamented, 'I'm going, lads. This is for mugs. I can earn twelve pounds a week in Coventry and that's for only fifty hours. Three pounds to your Uncle Joe and I've still got almost a tenner left in my arse pocket. Now you can't blame me, William, can you?'

'Not at all, but you'll be back, Gougho, that's if you go at all.'

'I'm going and I won't be back. By Jaysus, you can be sure of that.'

William thought that Gougho was only romancing, but three weeks later he shook our hands.

'I'll come and see you lads when I visit home,' he promised and was gone.

Molly had left home after marrying Seymour Shields at Glassdrummond Church. William was happy for her to marry the courteous and successful young farmer. Violet had left school and worked at Parkes, the high-class grocers in Markethill. Closing-time was eight o'clock but after tidying the shop it was nine before she finished and rushed home to meet Billy Beggs. After a dab of rouge on her cheeks and a comb through her hair, she would hand over the two shillings she gave me for cleaning her high-heeled shoes and they would head off to the dance. Billy, her only boyfriend, looked like the handsome young men depicted in her romance magazines, and from the time they met they stayed together.

The Hunters' farm being two miles away meant Aunt Ruth's visits were infrequent, leaving us to get on with our lives. Possessed of endless energy she easily coped with her farm chores and family duties; nearby Mount Norris village felt her presence too as she organized functions, badgering residents into attendance. Violet and I were always pleased to be invited but local folk were less keen.

'What do you mean, you're too busy and can't make it,' she said one day. 'Surely to Christ you'll come. And stop off at our house on the way to collect the cakes our Betty has made. Poor girl, she's worked her fingers to the bone.'

The annual Church dance was on that night, with lots of food and orange drinks. It was not until I saw Cousin Ruth, a lanky girl of about ten, selling tickets that I realized there was a raffle on. After parting with my two-shilling piece I enquired what the first prize was.

'It's a rooster, John,' said Aunt Ruth. 'One of my own.'

My aunt was an excellent poultry breeder so I knew it would not be a scrawny specimen. Most of her fowl had a sprightly strut. In the small room at the side of the hall Cousin Ruth and I counted the money and put the tickets into a basket. I wanted that rooster. All our hens had long since gone so he wouldn't have any company, but I could look after him and at last have something of my own.

'How can I pick your ticket out, John? We've got to mix them all up,' complained Ruth.

'My ticket is white, it's four one six and it'll be at the top with the number showing,' I told her repeatedly.

'Me Mammy will kill me, John, please don't make me.'

At midnight the band stopped playing and I carried the basket up to the stage where Aunt Ruth proudly announced that her wee girl had sold all the tickets and would pick the winning numbers. Nervously Ruth handed the first ticket to her mother.

'Number four one six,' my aunt called, her eyes scanning the room.

I waited.

'Come on, now, someone must have it. Doesn't anyone want a rooster?'

'Look, I've got it, Aunt Ruth,' I shouted.

'Oh well done wee John.'

'Where is he?' I asked.

'Sure I couldn't bring him with me, could I? I'll bring him to your house.'

A few days later she arrived with not only the rooster but half a bag of chicken-feed as well. An old hen-house remained in the buttercup field where I had celebrated my sixth birthday and he lived there for a few months before he progressed to the run of the yard. He grew into a fine big fella, almost turkey-size, with shiny red-brown feathers. Uncle John Hughes was always very suspicious of him.

'He seems a bit of a funny hure to me, I haven't heard him crow yet,' he remarked critically.

Why my new pet took such a dislike to Violet was a mystery to me. When she rode her bicycle into the yard he flew at her, pecking furiously at her legs.

One day Mrs Goodfellow was in the scullery when I came home from school.

'By Jaysus, there'll be a big feed on Sunday, John,' she laughed. 'Look up here,' and she pointed to the rafters in the corner of the scullery. There he was, hanging by his legs, his large wings outstretched in glorious splendour, congealed blood darkly marking the hole through his head.

'Why did you kill him, William?' I yelled.

'Why? Just go and look at Violet's legs.'

The lonely stillness of the house lifted only when visitors called. Sometimes Molly and Seymour brought their pretty baby girl Barbara and if they went for a walk I was trusted to look after the blonde curly-haired toddler. I was often left alone in the house at night, which I didn't mind because it gave me a chance to handle the single-barrelled shotgun I always wanted to fire. Summer was almost over and soon I would be back at school. Already my brothers were wearing donkey-jackets in the morning to stop the bite of the blustery north winds.

'*Cuckoo – cuckoo.*'

I ran along the lane to meet George Gardner.

'Still on holiday, are you, son?'

'I'm back in two weeks.'

'Give these to your brother,' he said, handing me three letters. 'So long now, cuckoo, cuckoo.'

The first letter in a brown envelope said 'W. A. Hughes, Lisnagat, Co. Armagh'. The second I recognized easily, a cheque from the Milk Marketing Board. The final one was a square white envelope addressed to William. My stomach started to heave with fear because I knew it could only be the school report I had dreaded for months. Weak-legged I walked slowly to the back yard where he was working.

'I think you've got a cheque, William.'

'About bloody time,' he growled, as he shuffled the letters through his large hands.

'I'm cleaning the concrete walk at the side of the byre for you,' I said cheerily.

Already he was staring at the white envelope. I found it difficult to concentrate and brushed the same place back and forth – waiting. Hours seemed to pass. Perhaps it was not the report after all, or maybe he wouldn't hit me too hard because I had worked well all week. I fumbled about with the brush then heard the slap-slap of his wellingtons. He had a look of dark intent on his face.

'Come 'ere,' he barked.

I dropped the brush and sidled forward along the wall.

'Closer, come on, over here.'

The white letter was in his hand.

'How the hell do you think I'll ever look at any of those teachers again? I'll have to walk on the other side of the street in Markethill if I see them. Not one of them has anything half decent to say about you. Listen to this one, "John is a disturbing influence on the class."'

Holding my hands against the back of my head I cowered against the wall. The blows, slow at first, increased as his temper boiled. I squealed and cried, 'I won't do it again, honest I won't, please, William.'

Feeling dizzy, I slumped down and he stopped.

'No good will ever become of you. You're not worth feeding,' he spat, and turned away.

I lay by the byre, memories flashing through my mind. I was a small boy again. William lay on the trailer and told me he was going to die. I begged him not to. Sombre-faced, he took his money and penknife out of his pocket and carefully laid them down on the trailer.

'I'm leaving my things to you, Bat, I'm dead now.'

In panic I furiously banged his chest.

'Please, William, don't die.'

When he opened his eyes and smiled I was so happy that I followed him around for weeks in case he died again. Images of my father and mother went as quickly as they came; the story father had told me of when late one night he had knocked on Uncle John Hughes's door. When it

99

opened he found the tubes of a double-barrelled shotgun pointing at him. Aunt Lucy was behind the door, Uncle John in the dark of the scullery, alert to the dangers of republican intruders.

I felt a surge of lonely anger and rebellion. Getting up I grabbed a four-pronged fork and ran, screaming, 'Come on, you bastard.'

William turned around. I had jabbed him before I knew it. Thick layers of clothes and a donkey-jacket checked the thrust of the blunt steel. I stood with tears pouring down my face, legs apart, shouting, 'I don't give a fuck if you kill me.'

Winded and visibly shaken he managed a mocking laugh, 'So Lippy has some guts after all, has he?'

My tears finally stopped, but I sat for a long time. Although only fourteen I knew I was a man and notions about leaving were clogging my head. Farm idiot, that's what I am going to be if I stay here, I thought.

'I'll have 'im, when I whistle he'll dance,' William boasted.

If I stayed how could I earn a living? Would he let me keep the money if I got a job? That day I made up my mind that somehow I would escape.

The following Saturday, having scrounged money from Joe, I went to see a film in Markethill. *North to Alaska* told the story of three cowboys and their search for gold. One scene showed them crossing the Yukon river, the horses' hooves whipping up a foaming spray around their legs. The music heightened and my stomach heaved.

Way up north, way up north,
North to Alaska, go north, the gold rush is on.
Big Sam left Seattle in the year of 'ninety-two,
With George Pratt his partner and brother Billy too,
They crossed the Yukon river and found the bonanza gold.

Ignoring the rest of the film, I raged and burned inside. It was difficult not to get up and leave there and then. I stared at the wooden walnut support framing the top of the seat in front of me. William, Joe and I were the three partners. I was brother Billy riding behind. When their backs were turned I would ride off to a different place. For a year or so now I had thought of nothing but independence, of making good, of supporting myself. My fantasies' wanderings showed me returning home at eighteen to a hero's welcome, neighbours and relatives smiling with pride as they shook my hand.

'Jaysus, will youse look at 'im.'

'Hasn't he changed.'

'You speak different to us now.'

'You've done so well, John.'

'Tell us, how the Christ did you manage it? Your father would've been proud of you.'

William was grinning and called me John.

'Well, I never thought I'd see the day,' he said, his hand outstretched. 'Leave it there, John.'

I looked smart in my suit, almost as tall as William now. Shaking his hand I made sure he felt the strength of my grip. No longer would he hit me, nor did he want to. Aunt Ruth and family were crowding around me, saying, 'Jaysus, John, it's great to see you again.'

I did not know the film had ended until the people in front stood for the national anthem. Rubbing the dampness from my nose with the sleeve of my school blazer, I heard Bob McClure, a neighbour's son, say, 'What are you snivelling about?'

'It's the smoke, Bob, it's making my eyes run.'

'Do you want a lift home on the tractor?'

'No, I've got to meet William.'

We joined the bustling queue to leave the cinema. Outside it was raining and a cold wind cut up Keady Street. William's car was gone.

'Are you going next week?' Bob asked.

'Yeah, I'll see you then,' I said quickly, wanting to be left alone with my thoughts. 'Goodnight, boy.'

In the kitchen the fluorescent light hurt my eyes.

'Why didn't you wait for me, William?'

101

'Sure I saw you with Bob McClure, I knew he'd take you home. Well, I'm going to bed, be up for Sunday school in the morning.'

Sitting by the table I stared into the spongy holes in a crust of bread. England, that is where I'll go, Uncle Joe will take me, I decided. He's got a lodging house, Gougho, George and Fran are there, and I get along well with Cousin Joe – he's always pleased to see me when he comes home. I'll save the fare. Gougho said it was about eight pounds on the boat. Then there's the train fare from Heysham to Coventry, and a feed as well. I'll have to save hard.

I felt the plan was sound. I was due to leave school in the summer just after my fifteenth birthday and uncle always came in July. To get the money was no bother, I could steal it from William.

Twelve

❧

Back at school I felt lonely without Violet. The work seemed so pointless now that I'd made up my mind to leave, so I took to clock-watching much to the annoyance of the teachers.

'Get on with your work, Hughes, the bell will tell you when it's time to go.'

Cousin Betty settled into her secretarial job in the new school. Her office window faced the main gates and when I was late she would point sternly at the clock, urging me on with a furious beckoning. Having access to the school files, she expressed concern over my report.

'You must try harder, John, you're letting mammy and your sister down. How do you expect to find a job with poor reports?'

A vivid imagination provided escape and I daydreamed for hours. What does Viral Pneumonia look like? I wondered. Will I know it if I see it? Perhaps it's a fungus that grows on floors or walls. It might even be small worms or insects. Insects? Yes, it probably is. Of course, that's why the vet gave father powder to dust on the walls, but surely they could not be there now after all this time?

Well over three years had passed since we last kept pigs. What would happen if I got a pig and she died? It was a chance I would have to take. I would know how to look after a sow and if she had a good litter I'd make a rake of money.

How long will it take to find a job? I asked. How much could a fella earn? Uncle Joe will want board money, he won't keep me for nothing.

These questions tormented me as I went into the best pig-house in the yard. Face up to the grey stones all I could see were beetles, wood-lice, flies and shrivelled left-overs in spiders' webs, the stillness disturbed only by the occasional knock of a bumble-bee. After brushing the floor and walls briskly with a yard brush, I bucketed water from the concrete trough by the shuck and dowsed the floor.

William surprised me. 'What are you doin', boy?'

'Just givin' this piggery a quick lick over.'

He glared around slowly.

'What put this notion in yer block? If you made as good a job of the byre your time would be well spent.'

'Can I have a pig?' I asked.

'A pig, no less! Ah, so that's what the crack's about. Where're ya gonna steal that from?'

'I've got some saving stamps.'

'How many?'

I hesitated. 'I'll have to count.'

'There could still be that disease in them oul walls,' he warned.

'Well, I can't see it,' I replied, refusing to be discouraged.

'Holy Jaysus Christ Almighty, are you a complete eejit altogether?' he sneered.

'But I thought ...'

'Thought my arse. Thought pissed the bed and thought he was on the pot. It's a virus, you can't see it. Still, it was a brave time ago, it might have gone – but don't cod yourself, if your pig gets it I'll be ringing Vercers.'

My mind flashed back to the death-wagon, the bluish stiff pigs, and the black dog.

'Well, count your stamps, you'll need about six pounds. When I'm in Markethill I'll buy you a runt and seeing you're at it make a start on the byre when you're finished here.'

I didn't want a runt, I wanted a real pig. A York like my father used to have, not a Landrace because Uncle John Hunter said they were prone to coughing. Most of all I wanted our Joe to buy it for me. He was good at dealing, father always said so. I was glad William had not insisted I count my money. If short of a few bob where could I say I got the rest from? He would suspect I'd stolen it, and anyway I didn't trust him with my money. Years before I had loaned him a ten-shilling note for a bet on the Grand National but poor Devon Loch, the Queen Mother's horse, had fallen on the run-in. He never repaid me.

That evening Joe took a look and seemed impressed.

'Just the hammer, boy, but lift that straw and if you go into the oul byre there's half a bagful of deep litter peat. Break it up and shake it round the floor, then the straw on top. And block up them holes with bags, sure the poor crater'll freeze to death. There's a few of them concrete blocks sittin' there doin' nothin' behind the dunkle wall. Put them up against the lip of the dure. The rats round here will ate the place down. Did our fella say you could have one?'

'Well, he didn't seem to mind.'

'How many shillings have you?'

'How many do I need?'

'Well, I mind the time four pound would get a brave pig but by Jaysus it's a bold man would have the neck on 'im nowadays. You don't want an oul crock so you'll be lukin' at six or seven anyway. Can you run to that?'

'Yes, I think so.'

'Christ, there must be a loughful of coppers in mineral bottles!'

'But sure I found some at the crossroads after the game on Sunday.'

'You mean the shiny fellas you and Patsy kicked into the grass?'

I said nothing, letting Joe believe that this was the source of my income. My intentions scared me, I needed to confide in someone but felt sick at the thought of being found out. William would thrash me. Helping Cousin John to feed their pigs one evening I noticed several Landraces coughing.

'Yer Da's right, Landraces do cough a bit.'

'Maybes they do but they're leaner. You get more money for a Landrace than for a York. It's better bacon.'

'Well, I won't chance one.'

'What do you mean, boy? You're not havin' a pig, are you? Where will you get the meal from?'

'Will you give me a drop?'

'Well yes, but if my Da catches me he'll choke the neck off me. They've told me to watch you, it's still the talk of the house, you and Slithery with them flowers.'

Now I was even more worried. If I didn't tell John he would keep asking.

'If I tell you will you get me the meal?' I asked.

'I'll get it for you anyway. Come on, tell me, you know you can trust me.'

Shaking his head John said, 'By Jaysus, I wouldn't chance it. William'll take the skin off your back.'

'I know, please don't tell him.'

'Stop worrying, will you?'

Somehow I felt braver now, very excited, eager to the point that I could hardly wait for Sunday morning. William went drinking in Markethill on Saturday nights and lay in on Sunday mornings. It was my best chance.

I was up early and knew it would have to be quick. The green trousers lay in a crumpled heap on the bedroom floor. Pretending to search for my best clothes which still hung in his wardrobe, I glanced nervously towards the bed. Only the top of his head was showing above the red eiderdown. The once-white lining of his trouser pocket was a dirty grey. Pinching the edge of a half-crown I slid it slowly out, careful not to let the coppers drop down with a telling clink. It was easy. I was away and off to Sunday school; but why wait for Sundays. I was good at it and enjoyed the thrill. I decided that if his pocket were only half-full I would take a tanner or a shilling, but if it were full, like this morning, then I would go for the half-crowns.

I had located my hiding-place already. If William found the money I was as good as dead. The red mansion polish tin fitted snugly into a hole in the wall of the old piggery near the makeshift toilet. With a stone put back on top it was safe. I felt pleased but I knew William was cunning and sharp and the slightest mistake could mean detection. What if he saw me coming out of the pig-house? To cover my tracks I placed a tin of air-gun pellets on a shelf on the opposite wall.

'Well, I keep my pellets there so's I can pick them up on my way down Seaboughan Lane when I fetch the cows,' I'd say if he spotted me.

After three weeks I had stolen just over two pounds.

'Have you counted them stamps yet?' Joe asked.

'Yes, and the cash, but I've got to get the money for the stamps yet.'

'Well, go and get it. You either want a pig or you don't want a pig. I'll have a luk in Tuesday and see what I can see, there's sometimes a brave clatter then. If not, Friday, the place should be teeming with them,' he said.

After school on Monday I cashed the stamps at the post office and gave the six pounds to Joe.

'Have you told William yet?' I asked.

'Give over, will you, I'm not tellin' him nothin', sure we haven't nothin' yet.'

Joe came home late on Tuesday, but the little trailer was empty. He waved me down as he got out.

'Now don't ate the face off a man, they were nothin' but a shower of skittery-arsed crocks. You can have your money back till Friday,' he said.

'No. No, you keep it.'

I knew it was safe with Joe. He wouldn't drink or gamble it.

'How's he gonna feed the frigger anyway?' asked William.

'Well, he's got enough for half a bag of meal.'

'Has he now, by Christ?'

William's look of curiosity worried me.

'Sure if he boils some of them oul spuds and champs the lot up he'll get by,' replied Joe.

'Kiss my arse, will you, it's bad enough feedin' him, he'll ate us out of house and home, never mind the bastard pig.'

'Ah give the garcon a chance, will you, he'll have to find something sometime.'

William left and I said nothing about John Hunter's promise to get me some meal. On Friday Joe was home early. I knew he had got her because as the car stopped, the trailer kept rocking.

'There you go, now, there's the makings of a fine sow.'

She was bigger than I expected and very lively. Excitement gripped me. I was as good as on the boat.

'Where's the meal, Joe?'

'What do you take me for? Sure I'd to put almost a pound myself to 'er. Seven pounds that gruntin' hure cost.'

'Holy Jaysus, now what will I do?'

'You'd believe anything,' he laughed. 'I'm only coddin' you, it's in the boot.'

'I'll do your shoes for you on Saturday, Joe, honest I will.'

'You will well, and help with the reddin' up, we'll be making a man out of you one of these days. I'll bring the trailer round, so go and open the door.'

She was happy to go into the house I had prepared, and golluped the warm meal down. William mouched out for a look and seemed pleased.

'Fine-lookin' pig, fine-lookin' pig. Well, at least you won't have time to go plundering people's gardens now,' and laughing he wheeled away, hands sunk deep in his blue dungarees.

At nine o'clock Joe came out to find me sitting on my hunkers talking to her.

'Surely to Christ you're not going to sleep with her? Come on, leave her, she's in good form.'

Uncle John Hughes looked her over and enthused, 'Jaysus, you'll be a farmer yet, boy!'

She soon grew into a big strong sow, fed every morning and evening on a mixture of meal and left-over scraps. Nothing went to waste but eventually with meal dwindling and the potato stocks low, I depended on Cousin John coming each Sunday with his parents. In the back of their old green Vauxhall he would have the quarter-bag of feed.

'John and I are going for the cows, William,' I'd say.

'Right, but no shooting and don't be all day about it either.'

Out in the yard John would creep to the car boot and grab the bag and we would hide it in the deep litter house. That would keep her going for a couple of weeks.

I think Patsy was a little envious of my pig. One Sunday when everyone was out of the way, we pretended to be pig farmers. We enjoyed playing at being men, walking round the yard chewing bits of straw.

'You've got a pig I hear for sale, Johnny,' said Patsy through clenched teeth.

'Ay, that I have but I'll take no less than thirteen pounds for her.'

'Thirteen pounds! By Christ she'd have to be a bold pig to want that much.'

Looking over the door, Patsy nodded his head, continuing to chew the straw.

'We'll have to weigh her first, Johnny.'

'Well, hold your horses, Pat, and I'll fetch the weighbridge.'

Neither of us knew how to work the contraption.

'Here,' said Patsy, acting out his part, 'come out of the way will you, I've been doing this for years.'

Pushing down the handle that locked the door he failed to position it securely, and the metal bar whipped up into his face just above his eye. He stood still for a few seconds, his hand clasped to his head. When he removed it, blood gushed down the side of his face. I was terrified. Never before had I seen Patsy so still and so white. 'I'd better go home, boy,' he whispered and was gone.

That night Patsy went to bed with his cap on so that his mother wouldn't see but the next morning the cap and Patsy were stuck to the pillow and all three were taken to the doctor. Francy and Mrs Goodfellow said we both needed our heads looked at.

'If it's not magpies' nests it's flowers and now bloody weighing machines. Jaysus Christ, when are youse goin' to get some sense, the pair of you,' they said.

When William saw Patsy he laughed.

'Could you weigh a pig for me, Slithery?'

'I could well,' growled Patsy.

One evening he took me by surprise.

'Would you sell the pig, boy?'

'Go away with you, you're coddin'.'

'No, honest to God, I'll give you thirteen quid for her.'

'Where did you get thirteen quid from?'

'I can get it, me Da says I can have her. He'll make a wee house.'

'No he won't. She's stayin' in my wee house.'

'Well, I tell you what I'll do with you, boy, I'll give you thirteen pounds and my sixteen mineral bottles.'

'Sure but you've no tops to them oul bottles.'

'I'll get you the tops.'

'Na, I couldn't sell her.'

'How about thirteen pounds, sixteen mineral bottles and I'll give you my two guinea-hens as well.'

'Fuck off, will you? William would shoot them, and where would you get the food for her?'

'Sure where are you getting yours? You must be robbin' someone blind.'

'Not me, Patsy,' I said, but he didn't believe me.

'Not half, John, I know you!'

His sister Bridget was courting John Evans and I often asked him to get me a ride in the back of John's old van.

'Meet, meet,' came Patsy's call.

'I can't, I've got to feed my pig.'

'Come here, will youse,' said Patsy, sidling down the field. 'I've got a desperate deal for you. Thirteen pounds, sixteen mineral bottles, my two guinea hens and a ride round Markethill in John Evans's van.'

'Christ, it's tempting.'

'Will you or won't you, then?'

'I can't, Patsy.'

'Ah well, there's nothing more a person can offer,' he said dejectedly, and went without even a goodbye.

Time dragged by but at last my sow was ready for servicing.

'Best leave her another day,' advised Joe, 'then I'll take her to Eddy Marshall's. It costs a quid. You haven't got it, have you?'

'No, Joe.'

I think my brothers were impressed by how I had managed so far. The service went well and she caught first time. I often rubbed her belly and wondered how many were in there. With help from John Hunter, Patsy and my own light fingers I provided for her as best I could. Near pigging time William began to take an interest in her and I became more than a little anxious, constantly reaffirming that she was mine.

'Sure no one's touchin' yer oul sow,' he growled.

Her time was almost up and Joe put her in a pen in the old kitchen, helping me to rig up three heat lamps which rayed on her back. Raising her head she stared at the low flaking ceiling and, grunting discontentedly, rubbed her side against the rough-sawn timbers.

'Are yer listenin', boy?' asked Joe. 'If she starts and I'm not here you've seen us do it before. Put the protector block over her neck. Boil the bottle and scald the scissors each time. Leave an inch of cord to the young 'un and hold the ends till the blood stops and watch her when she turns. If she can't eat them then she might smother them. Try and turn her so the teats are exposed, and if she won't feed use the sucking bottles.'

As it turned out, both my brothers were away, but I had no need to worry, she was the best sow I'd ever sat with.

'Seven little pink fellas. Ah well, it's a wee litter,' said Joe.

'She must have caught Marshall's boar at the wrong end of the day.'

My second school report arrived but I wasn't so frightened this time. I had become more confident, possibly in a strange way, through not worrying about being beaten. This time I watched William open the envelope. If I was in for a hiding then I wanted to get it over with quickly.

One teacher had written that I did not care and he was right. I had more important things to worry about now. The pigs were growing fast and trying to feed them was proving difficult. They just ate and ate, always hungry. I started begging pig-meal from a boy at school and somehow William found out.

'Apples and pears for pig-meal, what's it comin' to? There's no shame in you, is there?'

The beating was not as bad as the one when I jabbed him with the fork, and I had hardened. I needed the pigs and they had to eat. When Uncle John Hughes bought me a bag of meal out of his winnings on a horse, I could hardly believe my luck. William said he must have gone soft in the head.

Every day I passed the big potato field by the river on the way down Seaboughan Lane. The brown heads were dropping and dying so I had to take my chance soon. Stealing was easy and I left no signs, lifting only one stalk from each drill. Stooped under the weight of my sack I tramped heavily up the rutted lane, cursing bad luck to all cows when I slipped on a caked cowclap. I wanted to rest awhile but was urged on by whisperings among the shadowy trembling branches. I stopped to change shoulders, frightening myself as I made my final scramble.

'Quick, Tom the Devil's behind you.'

By the dunkle wall a dim light cheered me, outlining Spot sitting in a shiver.

'Come on,' I said, but he wouldn't move.

'Rats, rats,' I whispered and my little friend darted into the deep litter house, while I fumbled for the light-switch. A rat scurried for cover – too late. My little assassin was rarely beaten.

'Where have you been till this hour?' said William, his face flashing dangerously from me to the green-faced clock above the range.

'Ratting with Spot.'

'Get a few, did you?'

'Four.'

'Good, that's four less then.'

I slept peacefully that night knowing that there was mash for the morning.

'By Jaysus, they're comin' on fine,' was Uncle John Hughes's remark as he looked over the door next morning. 'You'll be able to stand us all a drink soon.'

'Don't encourage him,' said William, 'he'll get there soon enough. At least he hasn't the time to go dandering round the country with the slithery man. Up to no good, them pair, they couldn't be watched.'

I was dozing on the sofa one night waiting for the potatoes to boil for my pigs. Careful not to get caught, I made sure the stolen ones were at the bottom of the huge saucepan.

'What you doin', John?' William asked suddenly.

'I'm boiling my spuds.'

'Go on off to bed with you, son, I'll watch them for you.'

It was stupid, but his kindness brought on tears that would not stop and I cried most of the night. The next morning, up early for feeding, I wept again. He had mixed the potatoes with pig-meal and scraps of food.

Everything was going well and my sow moved to another piggery away from her young. It occurred to me that if they grew fast I might manage another litter before Uncle Joe came. Would there be time?

'Come on, fatten up for Jaysus sake,' I begged.

I decided to lift another sack of potatoes from the big field.

I was so happy that Kelly, the science teacher, was impressed with my sudden interest in learning.

'You see, you can do it if you want to, Hughes. It's still not too late.'

Webster was amazed to see me tearing round the gym eager to attempt all the exercises. 'Keep it up, Hughes, and you'll be in the school games next year.'

Betty must have reported to Aunt Ruth.

'Sure I knew you'd come good in the end,' my aunt said with a smile. 'You'll be leaving school in just over a year. One of these days I'll drop in to Hutchinsons in Tandragee and see if they'll take you on as an apprentice bricklayer.'

One morning I noticed some food left in the trough but decided I was overdoing it in my eagerness to get the pigs ready for market. I did not take much notice of the one that was wheezing slightly, until I saw Joe leaning over the piggery door.

'What's wrong?' I asked.

'Whisht a minute, will you. Listen. Can you hear it? There he goes.'

While he listened time seemed to fall away. I felt cold.

'It's back, boy, I'm tellin' yer.'

'Surely it can't be,' I said, not wanting to believe it.

Joe knew I was upset. 'Who would have believed it? It's a tarra, boy, but they'll have to go. It's Friday tomorrow, best day. I'll take them for you myself.'

'And the sow?'

'The lot. Here, let's get that one out of here. We'll put him in the oul byre. You're lucky I heard him, the rest are OK but they'll catch it as well.'

I went to school on Friday and watched the clock all day. When the bell sounded I cycled home as fast as I could. Joe was in the shed fiddling with the carburettor on the tractor. He glanced up then looked quickly away.

'How much did you get?' I panted.

'Our fella took them,' he splurted apologetically. 'He insisted, said he was going into Markethill anyway. Seventy-six pounds, I think. You've done well.'

'Can I have my money, William?' I asked, as soon as I saw him.

'Let me keep it until the end of the month. Until I get the milk-cheque. I'm a bit stuck at the moment.'

That night worry gnawed at my stomach and I could not sleep. The end of the month came, so did the next, and

William had more excuses. Twice I complained to Joe who eventually challenged him.

'Give the garcon his money, will you?'

'I will, I will,' promised William.

But he never did and now I wanted to hate him.

Thirteen

॰ঽ

The summer of 1961 was little different to any other, sunshine one day, howling gales the next, but the events of that year are deeply set in my memory, resurfacing occasionally to remind me of who I am and where I come from.

Still resentful towards William for keeping my money I continued to steal from him and as my confidence grew it became easier. I had opportunities to steal from Joe as well, but never did. My brothers had grown apart and although nothing was discussed in my hearing, I felt they had come to an arrangement, with Joe keeping his wages and the lion's share of the farm profits going to William.

I considered other ways of making money but decided it was useless trying to save openly for my future. William would just pocket the money anyway. In less than a year Uncle Joe would come and then I could escape.

Temperamental weather forced us to work at the harvesting until dusk and the shed was filling up with hay. William and Uncle John Hughes forked it up to where Cousin John and I stacked. We had great fun letting piles slip down, giggling and laughing as they cursed us.

'You buttery-fingered eejits. Are youse trying to kill us with the work?' they'd roar.

There were two light-bulbs in the shed. One was just above the door, in the middle of the wall separating the byre and shed, for illuminating a tunnel which was formed by stacking hay on either side. Fixed close to the roof was another bulb operated from the same switch. As the hay mounds rose, we were forced to kneel to avoid bumping our heads.

'William,' I shouted, 'no more up here, we're close to the light-bulb, it'll catch fire from the heat.'

'What would you know about it, give me none of your lip. I'll tell you when to stop,' was the only response I got.

Forkful after forkful, up it came.

'William, I'm tellin' you, we're near the bulb.'

'Do as you're bid, you gabby brat, do you hear me?' he growled.

'He needs to have a luk at this, John,' I said.

'I know, but sure you can't tell 'im.'

'Well, I'm gonna go down.'

'By Jaysus, you'll be back up a bit quick.'

Holding on to the tucks, I slid down the shiny bank gesturing with my hands. 'William, we're that far off the bulb.'

'Get back up there and let me hear not another word out of you,' he snarled as his hand smacked into the back of my head.

Furiously I made my way back up to John. He said nothing but had a knowing look on his face. Hot with embarrassment I attacked the crop, stacking it to the roof and trying to keep it away from the bulb. William was still scowling as we closed the shed doors.

'A few science lessons and he thinks he knows it all,' he sneered.

Within a couple of weeks I had forgotten all about my protest. William and I were sweeping the yard one Friday morning when Uncle John Hughes arrived.

'What are you doin' the morrow, William?' he asked. 'Are you goin' to tackle the Abbey fields or not?'

'May as well,' replied William. 'I looked at the heads on that corn the other day, they're hard as bullets.'

'Right you are. Me and our fella'll see you about nine.'

On Saturday morning, a fresh breeze hurried the clouds away across the sky.

'By Jaysus, Uncle John, she doesn't look too happy to

me,' said William, scanning the outlook.

'Ah come on, we're here now. If the rain chases us we'll find somethin' round the yard.'

Pulling into Kilcluney Rectory fields opposite Harold Anderson's I did not feel like working and already the day was dampening. The tractor struggled, causing deep ruts, eventually becoming bogged in a dip near the roadside hedge. After half an hour of pushing back and forth, we were out and on our way home.

'You can do nothin' in this country for the friggin' oul weather,' complained William. 'May as well sharpen the blades of the binder.'

'And that oul canvas could do with a luk as well,' replied Uncle John.

After dinner Joe went off in the car and in the early evening I fetched the cows home from Seaboughan and chained them in the byre. I went into the shed, where William and Uncle John were working on the binder. Before long the sky darkened as if it were dusk so we closed the doors and turned on the lights.

Encased by hay and old straw bales left over from last year's harvest, I sat on the chaff-littered floor watching them mend the machine, listening to the dull rasp of the file scraping against the blades. Huge fodder mountains surrounding us softened the light, and the steel members of the binder cast angular shadows which intensified a curious trembling within me. Raindrops pittered reluctantly on the roof, and a wind whistled under the galvanized doors. I gathered my coat closer; the scant light gave little comfort. I felt colder. There was something wrong, it was only summer yet I was shivering. The coldness was peeling my head. Leaning back, my knees held in the crook of my arms, I thought about going to throw darts in the byre where it would be warmer with the cows. Then I noticed something moving above me. I looked up. Smoke was curling and bending over the hay.

'There's smoke, there's smoke. William, we're on fire,' I yelled. His head jerked up. 'Jesus Christ – no, we are.'

There were sharp cracking sounds now, the smoke fast becoming a menacing cloud of fog almost enveloping the byre side of the shed. Panic gripped us as the smoke smothered the crisp air.

'It's the light-bulb, William, it's the light-bulb.'

'Open the doors, open them fuckin' doors,' he screamed.

A rush of wind sent the smoke swirling to the laneside division.

'Quick, the cows, Uncle John,' I shouted.

The smoke poured under the door, filling the byre in seconds. Roaring cows, wild-eyed with fear, strained against taut neck-chains, their hind legs stabbing and slipping in slurry as they fought desperately to free themselves.

'Get that back door open, John,' my uncle bawled, 'and watch your belly, they'll tear the middle out of you.'

We began unchaining, forcing our way between the hysterical beasts, always moving with them to avoid being slashed by their horns.

'Hold up a minute, will youse,' I yelled.

There were two more to go but Nancy and old Willow were wedged in the door, bellowing in terror.

'John,' uncle shouted, 'get a hold of that brush, go round and batter their heads.

I tore round the ribbled path. Nancy was almost out, her bulging eyes as big as apples. Frantically I stabbed the bristles of the brush into old Willow's nostrils.

'She won't go, Uncle John, she won't go.'

'Hit 'er a clout, will you, for God's sake.'

Reckless now, I turned the brush and smashed the wooden side into her nose. She jerked and twisted away, then crashing out of the gap, they both careered off in opposite directions.

'Go and chase them like the devil, John,' said uncle, his fingers jabbing. 'Anywhere away from here.'

There was no need to go further than the old flax-hole, where they huddled under a hedge by the side of the ragweed field, roaring and snorting, their tails slashing. Bolting back to the yard, I could see the red heart glow of the fire through the mouth of the hay-tunnel.

'Where in the name of God is it coming from?' begged William.

'I'm tellin' you, it's from ...'

As he twisted towards me my hand flashed up to cover my head.

'He's right, boy,' snapped uncle, 'it's the bulb.'

'Fill them buckets, youse two,' ordered William. 'Here, someone, give me a hand with this hose.'

'Open the windows, we'll choke in here,' gasped Uncle John. 'Come out the way, William, let us fill the buckets, will you?'

'Holy Christ, do as you're bid,' William roared at me.

Snarling with fury he told us to open the dividing door, then bawled, 'No, don't, hang on, where's the hose?'

They managed to attach the hose to the standpipe by the engine room and William rushed past Uncle John as he opened the door. A burst of blazing hay cascaded over him, sending whirls of embers sequinning into the air. Backing away, we aimed our water at the base of the fire. William, his face distorted, tried once again to get closer with the hose but it was hopeless. The thin jet was lost and the fire, growing rapidly now, switched to where it chose. Our eyes were melting with the intense heat. Suddenly a ball of flames roared down the tunnel towards us.

'Get to fuck out of here,' screamed William.

Stumbling into the byre we slammed the red-hot doors closed. A rush of smoke smothered us jamming our throats. Sharp cracking like rifle-fire made us twist and jerk. William was near to tears.

'Oh my Jesus, no, she's givin' in.'

As his words died a wide crack snaked down the byre wall.

'The electric, Uncle John, the electric. Get Jacky Love and the fire brigade,' he cried.

Soon a stern-faced Jacky raced into the yard, gripping a pair of wire clippers.

'Where's the fuse box?' he shouted, then cutting the wires, he gasped, 'at least the house is safe.'

Tyres screeched as Joe braked into the yard, followed by a fire engine. Men, in shiny black, were out before the machine stopped.

'Are the cows out?' Joe demanded.

'They're away,' William spluttered, 'but the byre wall's cracking.'

'Where's the well, boy?' spat a fireman. 'We've hardly any water.'

'Here, with me, come on,' shouted Joe, running through the byre and wrenching open the engine-house door. 'In there, the tank's at the top. Have you cut the wires, Jacky?'

'I have, Joe, the house should be safe, but we're in the hands of the man above now.' Joe's voice was fierce. 'Well, I hope He's lookin' down.'

'Hey boy,' he called to a fireman, 'mind that tractor, she's full to the brim of diesel, put a hose on 'er.'

'Right you are, boy.' Black-faced, another fireman burst out of the byre, yelling, 'We're running out, she's drying up. Is there a river?'

'Come here with me,' Joe shouted, already making towards the ragweed field. I followed.

'Sure the hose won't reach her,' said the blackened man.

Looking up the field I could see a cumbersome figure blundering down with another hose. The connection was quickly made.

'I can take them, Joe,' I pleaded. 'Honestly I can.'

He looked me hard in the face.

'Follow John,' he said, and vanished into the shadows before the flames.

Filled with fear and importance, I darted like a snipe through the ragweeds and thistles.

'Slow down, for God's sake,' came the plea from the two men.

When we reached the hedge that separated Henry Clarke's field from ours, the smaller of them tried to crawl under the barbed wire.

'Here, come round here, there's a gap at the side of this tree,' I shouted, and rushed back to the crowded yard.

Every neighbour I knew was there and some I didn't. I recognized the black car used by Constable Bertie Henry and Sergeant Campbell. Two more fire engines from Armagh had joined the Newtown Hamilton crew. The fire had become an inferno. Flames licked the galvanized sheets which cracked and split. Girders were bending; molten metal oozed from the tractor. Two shadowy figures, bent over, were pulling at bales of straw, jumping back as the flames threatened. I moved closer. It was William and Joe.

'Get out of there,' a fireman yelled.

They carried on. Another man with a pitchfork joined them. It was Molly's husband, Seymour Shields. At the top of the chestnut tree I could see the yellow glinting eyes of our Persian cat. Firemen continued to hose the tractor and I could just make out the charred form of the binder. I had not realized it was raining until someone shouted, 'God Himself is with us.'

'It's not through a want of time,' a voice retorted.

Not only was it raining, the wind had dropped as well.

There was a metallic clink and I turned to see a cloud of black flakes settling on the distorted frame of my bicycle. As I watched, another bike was hurled from the shed. It was Violet's. I felt empty as I gazed at the warped remains, wheels twisted, spokes missing, tyres gone, a strand of tape trailing from the handlebars.

The two policemen worked together forking out the black sodden lumps. Constable Henry removed his jacket, his white starched shirt turning a ragged patchwork grey.

'Thank the Lord,' he uttered, looking up.

It was raining fast now.

'Fuck the Lord! A lot of good he's done for us,' raged William and stormed off to the kitchen. Joe helped fix a wire rope to the tractor axle and a group of men hauled it out, the sickening stench of scorched rubber hanging in the air.

'He must be with us, Joe,' said Constable Henry again.

'If that tank had gone up we were all finished.'

'Well, someone needs to be with us.' Joe's voice was almost gentle.

Only a few metal sheets were left on the building now, the girders bent and bowing, some doubled over as if in agony. The first wet grimy men trudged out coughing and spluttering. Others surged forward, forking, tugging, throwing debris away from the blaze. The change was not in the darkness of the yard, it was in my eyes. Nothing was familiar. My stomach heaved and retched with hollow sickness. I could see waves of heat rising up the many windows of the house. In the reflections, eerie figures and grotesque objects cavorted in mirrors of flame. I wanted to see Mrs Goodfellow.

In the kitchen she was pleading with William to have a cup of tea.

'Please don't go out yet, William, sure you look done for.'

Steam rose from the sodden shirt clinging to his back like a wet creased canvas. Torturing his eyes with black fingers, he shook his head as if trying to waken himself. Half scared to look I risked a glance. There were tears on his face. His mouth hung open. The big man was crying. My despair deepened and I went back outside.

Suddenly fresh panic filled the yard.

'Holy Jesus, help us quick, will youse, he'll smother,' screamed an hysterical voice. 'He's gone down. It's Seymour. He's gone down.'

'Lemme by,' roared Joe.

As he scrambled up the sodden black bales, I could hear a faint desperate voice.

'Get me out, get me out.'

'Someone catch a hold of my legs,' ordered Joe. 'Grab my arm, Seymour, grab me.'

Slowly, coughing and spluttering, Seymour's head appeared for a second then sank again as the bales shifted. Amidst a shroud of burning smithereens, Joe cursed.

'Keep a hold of my legs, will youse,' and with a savage

roar he almost disappeared after Seymour.

'Pull! Pull!' came a muffled cry.

Seymour was out. They brought him into the yard, his streaming eyes like red marbles, his body racked with convulsions. In the kitchen Mrs Goodfellow sat with him till the coughing subsided and he was able to swallow a mug of tea.

'Holy Jaysus, Holy Jaysus,' he repeatedly coughed and slapped his knees.

'Will youse listen to it?' William snapped bitterly. 'There's another one wants to thank the man in the sky.'

Violet made sandwiches as fast as hungry men could eat them. The fire was under control now and they were able to rest awhile. The Newtown Hamilton crew pulled out, and William ordered me to bed, but I couldn't sleep. I wondered if the smoke and stench would ever leave. From the window I watched as the Armagh Brigade left. It was two in the morning. Heavy-limbed figures, boots scrunching, trudged wearily down the lane. No one spoke, no gesture, nothing. Closing the curtains I faced the wall and shut my eyes.

Daylight was breaking when William and Joe finally came to bed. Getting up I went out into the yard. A quietness hung over the twisted charred wreckage while cows roared nervously by the gate. They wanted milking. In the distance I could hear the church bell toll at Kilcluney. What would the Reverend Kerr say as he stood before the congregation that had stood by us the night before?

After lighting the range and boiling the kettle I woke William and Joe. William threw his long legs out of the bed, strode quickly to the window and snatched open the curtains. Staring out, his lips twisted inwards as he fought to conceal his emotions, but the tears rolled down his face.

'What will it be next, mammy's dead, the oul fella's gone and now we're burned to the ground.' He was openly crying now.

'Is the tay on, John?' Joe asked.

'She's about boiling,' I said, and went downstairs.

In a tremulous voice Violet offered breakfast, but no one wanted it and we supped our tea in silence.

'Them cows are roaring their heads off, boy,' said Joe.

'But sure they won't go into the byre,' moaned William.

'Then we'll milk 'em in the fields. Come on, they need it, they weren't done yesterday.'

The tragedy of the fire dominated our lives for many months afterwards. Mrs Goodfellow said the devil himself was in the place. Friends and neighbours shook their heads sadly.

'It's a holy tarra. As if you poor creatures haven't had enough already. It makes you wonder how He could allow it to happen.'

After a few days the cows were persuaded with the aid of sticks to accept the byre again.

The cleaning-up operations took months. Fodder and all kinds of machinery were loaned by Uncle John Hughes, the Hunters and sympathetic neighbours. When threshing was completed, the grain and straw were stored in disused piggeries. William seemed to relax more when the result of the insurance investigation arrived. He had wanted to cancel the premium in order to save money and only Uncle John Hunter's strongly argued intervention had kept the policy going. As it was, he was under-insured and received a cheque for only half the loss. A new tractor and binder accounted for a large proportion of the money, leaving barely enough to buy materials for a new shed. However, labour costs were drastically reduced when Jacky and Joey Love stepped in to assist Eddie McConnell, an experienced builder. Throughout the autumn this hardened crew, hands calloused and bleeding, erected a new building. Only one slightly bowed girder was reused, a rusting reminder of our ruin.

Of all the memories etched in my mind, one in particular shadows me. After the fire Uncle John Hunter quizzed William as to what might have caused it. William hedged and finally answered he wasn't sure. When I told uncle I thought it was the hay packed tight against the light-bulb, he threw his hands up in despair.

'Holy Jaysus, William, what were you thinking about?' he asked.

My brother looked painfully embarrassed and I knew then that I should not have spoken out. After this he beat me severely almost on a daily basis, often for no reason. Sometimes these thrashings to the head took place in front of neighbours or relatives, whose mild protests, 'Ah that's enough, Billy,' seemed almost to condone the violence. I became desperate to avoid being beaten, terrified that if it continued I would be in no fit state to go to England.

Christmas '61 passed uncelebrated, with not many cards or callers. It seemed to me that we desired and welcomed the bleak and lonely seclusion. No effort was made, no one wanted it to be any different. Dinner was a fry of bacon, potatoes and cabbage. Boxing Day, William, Joe, and the Love brothers took me shooting, roaming Seaboughan fields. Stillness lay heavy on the hedgerows. A curious robin eyed us with a lazy look, then hopped away behind a leaf of snow. Joey shot a blackbird that treated us with the same indifference. 'There's nothing out,' said William. We went home and huddled around the dying fire.

Only six months till Uncle Joe would be here. Thoughts of leaving school filled me with a nervous excitement. Realizing it was time to start stealing again, I resented my sympathy for William. Money was scarce, he had worked so hard. Let him get on his feet with a few milk-cheques, the lightness of spring would cheer him and it would be easier to dip in when he was happy.

One morning in the early spring of 1962 Uncle John Hughes, Cousin John, William and I were working in Seaboughan. Several hares bounded out of their hides and settled in a nearby meadow. William sent me home for the ·22. In the press drawer I found the buff-coloured box of bullets. Walking back along the lane, my steps shortened when I reached the river and I sat on a mossy bank cradling the rifle. My intentions did not scare me. I had decided to kill William and this was the best way. Now it was a matter of which angle to shoot from. I considered creeping along the hedges till I reached Seaboughan Hill. Then I would have a clearer view, but I remembered father always said a downhill shot was very difficult, often missing the target because of the backdrop. What if I missed or wounded him? I could not afford the risk so I settled for the flat angle. Tucking myself into the hedge opposite where he was working, I waited and, after what seemed like hours, he appeared and lit a cigarette. I felt calm as I placed a bullet in the rifle but the click of pulling back the bolt startled me. Resting the barrel on a branch I took aim and lined both sights in a perfect 'V' on William's forehead. But when the pad of my finger touched the trigger I began to shake uncontrollably. Carefully I moved my finger back and placed the weapon on the ground. The shaking continued but eventually with my composure semi-restored I made my way back to William.

'Where have you been, boy? Have you seen a ghost or something?' he asked.

After this I developed a strange inexplicable love for my brother, constantly wanting to be near him. I considered trying to prove my love by telling him I had spared his life but thought better of it.

Fourteen

It was a fine summer's morn-
ing. I rose earlier than usual. The tea tasted a little bitter
because there was no sugar so I poured it into the sugar
bowl, spooning it around the edges, watching the formed
clusters melt reluctantly. Stirring tea in a sugar bowl makes
a different noise than in a cup, grating and bumping in
agitated interference.

The sticky flycatcher was black with insects. Those that
were barely alive would soon fry once the range was lit. A
dozy bumble-bee desperately struggled to free itself so I
prised him gently off onto a match and took him outside to
the hedge. There was a sharp nip in the air; my bare feet
were tingling.

Back at the table I folded my fingers round the sugar
bowl. I heard Violet's footsteps. The sun struggled to clear
the wispy hedge and sent a warning flash through the faded
pink curtains. I averted my eyes.

'Hello, you might have made a start on the fire,' said
Violet with a wide yawn.

She's a lovely girl, my sister, I thought, even in the
morning. When I'm married I hope it's to someone as nice-
looking as her.

'Any tay left or has the tay-ginny supped the lot?' asked
William, flopping into a chair.

He seemed to be in a good mood but when his eyes
sharpened towards the sugar bowl, I looked away.

'Sweet enough for you, Lippy?'

'It'll do till you go shopping.'

He didn't seem cross.

'You'd cheek Old Nick himself, wouldn't you? No you wouldn't, he wouldn't have you down there. You've got to work in hell. Can't see you stoking fires. Are you going to be all morning sitting there? Get ready for school.'

My drop of tea had gone cold. Down the hall. Grip the rail. Up two steps. Suddenly my arm and hand were ablaze; so was the black bannister, raging red, firing spear-shaped flames. Firemen ran out of the room at the top of the stairs. They looked different to the ones I'd seen before. In tunics, with silver buttons and bucket-shaped helmets, holding small axes over their shoulders they thundered past, ignoring me. There were dozens of them, hurrying along in single file. They wouldn't help me, just kept going.

I felt strange, couldn't see straight.

'Please, I'm burning, and it's so hot,' cried a voice in my head.

'What happened, John?' said Violet's voice.

I was on the sofa now with a cushion under my head, and Violet was sitting by me. 'Nothing. I've got a sore head, it's hurtin',' I whispered shakily.

'So it would. You fainted. Had a turn and passed out. You've cracked your head on the tiles. No, lie still a wee minute.'

'I'm OK. Where's William?'

'Away for Aunt Ruth.'

'Can I have the day off school?'

'A few days, maybe. Here, drink this.'

'Where d'you get the sugar from?'

'I hid some in the press,' she said, with a smile. 'Now don't move till Aunt Ruth comes.'

'What will she do with me?'

'I don't know, I'm sure.'

A car swerved into the yard, braking fast by the hedge.

'Here's Aunt Ruth,' announced Violet, moving to the door. William rushed in, slowing before me. White taut face. His eyes looked bigger.

'How do you feel, John?' he asked.

'There's nothin' wrong with me.'

Aunt Ruth came in, followed by Uncle John.

'How do you feel, wee John?' she inquired, pushing William aside.

'I'm alright.'

'What's your head like?'

'It's a bit sore but I'm alright, honest, Aunt Ruth, I am.'

She put her arm round me.

'God love you,' she said, quietly.

It was nice. Warm. She smelt of lavatory soap.

'Where's it hurt, son?'

'Round here,' I said, rubbing the back of my head.

'Jaysus, Daddy, will you feel the lump on 'im? Violet, where's his blazer? William, we're taking him straight there ourselves. I rang up before we left and they can see him this morning.'

They? Wonder who they are? I thought. Can't be Markethill. Must be Armagh or Portadown.

Violet looked sick. I'd never seen her brow so wrinkled before. William was quiet. I wondered what he was thinking. Aunt Ruth sat in the back of the car with me, her hands clasped round my elbow.

'Violet says I can stay off school for a week, Aunt Ruth.'

'Don't worry about school. Sure there's no need to hurry back.'

'It's science and algebra today, I'm no use at either.'

'Stop bothering your head, wee John. Sure I've come through life and I didn't know that a plus b equals c. A lot of good that oul codswallop'll do you. You're going to be a bricklayer, it's settled, I've seen Hutchinsons in Tandragee.'

I liked this conversation. Aunt Ruth was agreeing with everything I said. I wondered if she would get me a new bike. Uncle John was very quiet. He kept swallowing. We passed the Armagh turn and headed towards Portadown.

'Is it Portadown we're going to, Aunt Ruth?'

'No, son, we're taking you to Belfast.'

I shuffled away a little. Why Belfast? That was a big place.

'They need to X-ray your head.'

X-ray my head! That meant I was going to have my head looked at. Something leapt inside me. Everyone would know and talk about me.

'There's John Hughes, don't say I told you but he's away in the head.'

'You're coddin'.'

'Sure as you're standing here, I'm tellin' you, he's been to Belfast and had his head looked at. They all get sent there.'

Aunt Ruth moved closer, her arms around me.

'Wee John, I promise you it's nothing. They only want to see if you hurt your head when you fell.'

'Not long now, son, this is the motorway,' said Uncle John, glancing back.

'Has your John been along this road?' I asked.

'No, he hasn't, you've beaten him to it,' he said, smiling gently into the mirror.

'Will there be many there, Aunt Ruth?'

'It doesn't matter who's there, you keep with us, we're not going to be long.'

Not long. I couldn't be that bad, I decided. If I was, sure it would take ages.

'What happened this morning, John?' she asked, gripping my hand. I explained about the bannister, my arm and hand, the firemen.

'Their side was not burning, Aunt Ruth, but they didn't stop for me.'

The engine slowed and Uncle John squinted at me through the mirror, looking puzzled. We swerved.

'Jaysus Christ, you oul eejit, will youse look where we're going? Are youse tryin' to kill us?' snapped Aunt Ruth.

He coughed and swallowed again.

'God love us, Daddy, his father will be turnin'. Now tell me the truth, John, does them pair hit you?'

I didn't like this question. If I said yes it would go back and I'd get hammered. She repeated the question.

'Don't be feared. Tell your Aunt Ruth, are they rough

131

with you?'

'A wee bit.'

'A wee bit, my arse,' she said, talking to uncle. 'What do you think, Daddy?'

'Do you backchat them, John?'

'Sometimes,' I admitted. He frowned.

Bet he thinks I deserve it, I thought.

'Who hits you the most?' Aunt Ruth's voice had lost its urgency. She took a deep breath, her big chest heaving.

'Well, Joe's not too bad. Only when he loses his temper.'

'He takes after Granda Hughes for that,' she said apologetically. 'Is it the other fella then?'

'Yes.'

'By Jaysus, I'll kill 'im myself.'

'No, Aunt Ruth, he'll ...'

'He'll what? He'll not lift his hand to you again, I'll make sure of that. Where does he clock you?'

'Round the head, but I cover myself.'

Her hand stroked the back of my head.

'He wants to get someone his own match,' she shouted, looking anxious. 'Slow down, Daddy, I think it's left here. Why don't you come and see us more, John? You used to be down every week.' Here was my chance.

'I would, I like coming, Aunt Ruth, but I've got no bike.'

Her reply was instant.

'I'll get you and Violet new bikes.'

I felt happy, thinking, what about a pig? I could keep it at McCune's. I wonder would she? No, there's no point, I'm not doing all that again just for William.

Belfast was a bustle. It was eleven o'clock and there were people everywhere. A woman with a shawl and an oversize brown coat lunged, arms waving, at a bend in the road. Uncle blasted his horn.

'Jaysus, they're all out today.'

'I don't think that one is all there, Daddy.'

We stopped by the traffic-lights. A man was selling newspapers. I'd never seen that before. He looked like Fitzpatrick, only better dressed. A posh-looking man folded a paper and slid it into his pocket while the paper-seller held out his change with a limp arm, giving the posh man an impatient look.

'This is the Crumlin Road, John. Did you see the jail?'

'No. Where is it?'

'Back there. You haven't missed much. Some quare fellas in there, isn't there, Daddy?'

'There is that. All the rogues in the country.'

'Lots of traffic-lights, Aunt Ruth.'

'Sure they need them. Half the poor devils here couldn't cross the road without them.'

'This is it here, isn't it, Mammy?' said Uncle John, braking suddenly.

'Ay. I should take them big gates.'

'Where now?'

'Don't know, I'm sure.'

Well, I'll pull in here.'

'No, Daddy, that's reserved for doctors. Jaysus, John, I'll learn to drive myself one of these days.'

'You can start now if you want,' uncle grinned.

'Whisht a minute, will you, Daddy? Let me ask that wee girl.'

She leant over and I was squashed against the window. 'You wouldn't know where the EEG place is, would you?'

'Yes, surely. Through the big doors, take the corridor on the right, then there's another set of doors and it's the third room on your left – no, sorry, which way round am I, yes, on your right.'

'Lovely-looking girl, that one. Come on, son.'

Aunt Ruth had a look of determination about her now as she took my hand and led me through the doors into a wide hallway. Sickly yellow walls, soft green floor-covering. A doctor in a white coat opened the next door, smiled through stretched lips and beckoned us forward. Uncle thanked him but Aunt Ruth appeared not to have seen him. There was serious intent on her white face. She rapped on the door marked EEG, muttering, 'No one at home?'

Uncle looked embarrassed. It was opened by a very

young-looking doctor with a look of annoyance on his face.

'Yes? Good morning,' he snapped.

My aunt was not intimidated.

'I'm Mrs Hunter, the wee child's guardian. I rang this morning. Sure it's an awful thing. He's had a turn. On the stairs it was. Fell down and cracked his head. Feel the lump on 'im, it's as big as a turnip and I'm worried out of my skin.'

'Just a wee minute, Mrs Hunter, you want the specialist. Just sit yourselves down there,' the doctor said, more kindly, and disappeared, closing the door behind him.

Footsteps came to a halt outside the room and a fat-faced man came in, chollers quivering.

'Good morning, Mrs Hunter. I'm sorry you've been kept waiting,' he said, over-shaking my aunt's hand.

'We couldn't get here quickly enough, Doctor.'

'Tell me what happened this morning, John,' he said quietly.

I repeated all that went before. He frowned, shaking his head and tut-tutting a little. Aunt Ruth was bursting to talk.

'Sure you haven't heard the half of it. He's got no Mammy or Daddy, both went home, almost together, only seven months between them. Would you believe it and his father fit as a fiddle? But his Mammy, poor thing, she'd had it bad for years and just as they were getting on their feet – the fire. Sure they were lucky to get away with their skins. I'm not the better of it yet. Daddy and I, we're the guardians, but the brother's old enough now and rules the roost. But we do our best for them.'

The doctor divided his glance between us until he found a gap to speak.

'Well, what I'd like to do, Mrs Hunter, is complete an EEG. It won't hurt John, I promise.'

'Can she stay?' I asked nervously.

'Sure, I'll stay wee, John, I wouldn't leave you on your own.'

'Lie back here, son,' said the doctor, patting a narrow table.

The sheets were gleaming brighter than whitewash. He helped me out of my blazer while Aunt Ruth tried to take my shoes off. She looked a little embarrassed because she couldn't undo the knot.

'Here, Daddy, will you ...'

She changed her mind and yanked them off hard. I felt my toes catch on the inside. She passed the shoes without comment to uncle. He cradled one between his knees fiddling with it.

Aunt Ruth drew a chair up beside me. The doctor seemed concerned about her and told her not to worry. Her face was so white and her big blue eyes looked paler.

The nurse reminded me of Violet. She had a lovely face and smelt of flowers, roses, like the ones around our gable.

I heard clicking, then a low purr like the drone of a faraway thresher.

'There you go, Mammy.' Uncle placed the shoes under his chair. I could see his bald patch as he bent down. The nurse was holding a coil of wires that looked like giant daddy-long-legs, hanging from a hairnet. The doctor was talking to my aunt in a low tone.

'Watch the paper as it comes out. This machine measures the brain's electrical impulses.'

'God love us, what will they think of next? What am I looking for?'

'Regularity, Mrs Hunter. A pattern of lines all the same.'

The nurse put the wires around my head. I felt as if I were wearing a magpie nest.

'Are you alright, wee John?' Aunt Ruth asked. 'Don't worry, it's for your own good.'

Was it me or had it started? It was a funny feeling. Ticklish. I wanted to scratch my head. I wondered what the machine could see. The paper. What would it say? If it showed I was funny in the head, what would happen to me?

Aunt Ruth got up to watch the paper. Her eyes were watery. Her penetrating look swept slowly away from me.

'Don't worry, son, God save us.'

'Right,' said the doctor. 'Just here. Watch the pattern.'

I heard scribbling and occasional clicking.

Where have I heard that before? I wondered. Ah yes, in the school office when Cousin Betty was typing. I was worried now about the machine. I was determined to lie still and not get excited. In one of William's *True Detective* magazines I read something about a murderer in America who tried to beat a lie detector test by making himself stay calm. I held my breath. They wouldn't have got Harold Anderson in here. He would have seen them in his big mirrors. They'd be reading books and drinking buttermilk by now.

'Are you enjoying yourself, John?'

The nurse had caught me smiling.

'Well, that wasn't too bad now, was it?'

The noise stopped and she removed the nest. On with my shoes and blazer. I looked at the sheets of green checked paper but all I could see was a series of jagged lines.

'There is some irregularity here, Mrs Hunter,' said the doctor, pointing to one of the sheets. 'You can see how the zig-zag lines have altered over that small area.'

'Well, could that not be because of the fall now.'

'No, the fall was nasty but it is not related. This is something else. Come in here just a wee minute, will you?'

Uncle followed them into another room. He looked a bit concerned and Aunt Ruth's jaw had dropped and her mouth hung open. The nurse talked to me. She was nice, but I wished she would be quiet because I wanted to listen. Something about him looking thin. The door opened. It was the doctor.

'Helen, can you take John's weight?' and the door closed firmly again.

'Just step on here a wee minute, John. Here, let me slip your blazer off.'

'Six stone and three pounds,' she announced when the doctor reappeared looking impatient.

'Right,' and he was gone again.

'Just rest yourself here now, they won't be long,' said the nurse and I was left alone.

I felt scared listening but I wanted to hear.

'Why is he only just over six stone, Mrs Hunter? He's almost fifteen. A lad of his height should be about eight stone. Has he no appetite?'

'Appetite! Don't make me laugh. He'd ate a bullock if he could catch him. Sure Daddy, tell 'im about the turkey.'

Uncle started but wasn't allowed to get very far. Aunt Ruth explained how Cousin John and I ate her Christmas turkey.

'And then the pair of rascals had the neck to sit down with us.'

'What's his home life like?' the doctor asked in a low tone.

'Well, I suppose it could be better. I don't get up as much as I'd like to. The older sister is married. There's just him and Violet, who's out all day, and the two brothers. Sure them poor creatures are working themselves to skin and bone. Cooking would be the last thing in their heads. But he eats well at school. He's always got his dinner-money. I can tell you that for sure, my daughter works there. Marvellous job she's got. Secretary – more or less runs the place. Clever girl she is and works very hard. Sure I've done my best for her.'

'Mrs Hunter. Going back to the wee lad's home life, can you tell me … oh just a moment. Helen,' he shouted, opening the door. 'Oh she's gone. Would you like a cup of tea, John?'

'No, I'm alright, thank you.'

He closed the door again and I could hardly hear anything because they were talking so quietly. Uncle cleared his throat but didn't say much. I wished he would because he had a loud voice. I wished I'd had the tea now, my mouth was parched. It was longer than Sunday school. At last they appeared.

'I'll contact your doctor. Thank you for bringing him in so quickly.'

'Not at all. It's the least we could do.'

'Cheerio now, John, you're going to be alright but no

strenuous school games and try not to get too excited about things.'

Excited. If he only knew.

'Can I sit in the front, Aunt Ruth?'

'Surely you can. Alright, wee John, are you?' she said for the hundredth time.

Turning back onto the motorway it was quiet; the sky tried raining but decided to cheer us up with pale sunlight instead. The wipers left dirty smear-marks on the windscreen. Uncle looked for a rag but couldn't find one so he wound down the window and rubbed a patch clear with his cap. He was unsteady driving with one hand.

'Daddy, will you steer her not aim her, we're not ready to meet our maker yet.'

'Give over your blethering, will you. Twenty-one years I've been on the road.'

A skein of geese veered off high to our left.

'Look at them, Uncle John.'

'Jaysus, there is a brave oul clatter of them. You wouldn't get near them with a shotgun. You'd need William's ·22.'

Aunt Ruth leaned over.

'John, you haven't used your father's big gun yet, have you?'

'No, but it's my turn soon. When I'm fifteen Joe says he'll show me.'

'You mustn't touch her, John. I'll have a word with your fella.'

'Why not, Aunt Ruth?'

'Because, wee John, you're not well.'

'Is that what the hospital said?'

'Yes it is, and they know best.'

I felt very worried now. 'What's wrong with me, Aunt Ruth?'

'I'm not sure. It's something to do with the head.'

'What sort of something?'

'John, I'm not a doctor but there's something wrong that's not right, and while we're at it, you mustn't go swimming or climb up the haystacks, and keep off the tractor. No more driving.'

'I don't drive. I only had one go on yours.'

'And keep away from moving machinery, and stop getting so excited.'

I didn't feel excited now. Just a quiet darkness.

'You see, wee John, if you had another fit ... turn, I mean, you could get yourself kill't.'

'Fit!! What sort of fit? I don't have fits. Fits of laughing, maybes.'

In a heavy silence we turned off towards Portadown. Fits. I didn't have fits. I wished she would tell me. An angry hotness surged through me.

'Tell me, Aunt Ruth, tell me, will you, it's my head and it's not fair, I should know what it is.'

'Pipe down and don't you lose your temper with me. I'm trying to do my best for you.'

'Tell him, Mammy. He needs to know,' interrupted Uncle John.

'John, you have something they call Epilepsy. What it is exactly I don't know, but it could happen again. You've got to go on tablets.'

'What sort of tablets?'

'Oh Jaysus, how do you say the word, Daddy?'

She took a few stabs at 'Myso ... Myslin ... Mysoline, that's them. They're to cool you down, and you must take them twice a day until you're twenty-one. When the hospital gets in touch with the doctor next week, I will get them for you myself. Is it round here he hits you?' she asked, touching the back of my head.

'A bit sometimes.'

I was scared because I knew she was going to scold William. It was alright for her, she could leave but I would have to stay with him.

The car slowed to a stop in our yard. I wished this wasn't going to happen. William was in the kitchen gawking through the window but he didn't come out. Aunt Ruth stomped down the steps and her left shoe came off. Her eyes narrowed and fixed on the door. She fitted her shoe on again, clonked the heel on the concrete then flung open the green door.

'Hold your horses, Mammy, are you tryin' to bring the dwelling down?' asked Uncle John. 'Jaysus, wee John, there's going to be an almighty rumpus,' he whispered.

I stood by the press. There was a reluctant inquisitiveness on William's face.

'Put that over a chair.' She handed me her coat and threw her white handbag onto the sofa. William juggled mugs around the table. Sideways in a prowl she moved towards him. Uncle John had a coughing fit.

'Now just a wee minute, Mammy,' he spluttered but my aunt didn't hear. There was a wooden chair blocking her path. Her hand and leg moved quickly together pushing it aside. The grating noise startled William. Poker-faced, he froze.

'Never again, do you hear me? Never again will you lift a hand to that child.' Without turning, her right hand pointed back at me.

'You're far too heavy-handed, you oul brute, get some-one your own match. Try one of them boys in Markethill on Saturday night or would you need a bellyful of porter in you. And the same goes for the other fella, is he at work, yes? I mean what I'm saying now, do you hear me?'

Her finger wagged furiously.

'You can ring me if there's any more hitting, John.'

'Sure I've hardly touched him and when I do he asks for it,' said William, stepping backwards. 'You don't have to take his gab. If wastrels were scarce he'd make ten. I'm tryin' to keep this place on its feet and there he is not prepared to do a hand's turn. What's wrong with him anyway, did you find out?'

'He's had a bad turn. There's something wrong with the back of his head. He has to take tablets till he's twenty-one.' Aunt Ruth replied, moving towards the range. 'Fire out, is it? Have youse no coal?'

'I'll get it,' and I grabbed the shovel quickly. I was glad to get outside. She started again.

140

'You ought to be ashamed of yourself, William. Look at him, will you, sure there's more fat on a rooster. Once more, William, do you hear me, and there'll be someone here to see you. By Jaysus, if his daddy was alive you wouldn't touch him.'

The coal heap was low but I got what I could. Back inside they were all sitting down. Uncle was staring at the floor. I shovelled the small lumps into the range. Even the fire was timid, flickering weakly. Slag dust rose up, settling on the collar of William's drip-dry shirt. After a cup of tea, the Hunters got ready to leave.

'I'll see the doctor next week, John, and don't be putting racing handlebars on the bike,' warned Aunt Ruth.

'Having a bike, is he? Where's that coming from?' William's voice was subdued.

'From me,' said Aunt Ruth. 'Two Raleighs. I'll get them myself and don't bother your arse, it'll not cost you a penny.'

'Jaysus, Aunt Ruth, I'm only asking.'

'Well, just you make sure he doesn't put racing handlebars on.'

'Why's that, now?'

'Jaysus Christ,' she shouted. 'Because if he comes off of her or goes over the top his head will hit the road first.'

She enquired what time Violet would be home.

'Tea-time,' said William. 'Parkes is letting her off with a couple of hours.'

'So he should, the slave-drivin' oul prig. He's killin' the girl. Right now, I'll see you on Saturday, John. It might have to be a second-hand one. I'll have to see how far the money runs.'

'She's a fine-lookin' shed now, William,' remarked uncle, gladly switching the talk.

'She is that and she ought to be. Look at these.' William outstretched his scarred hands.

'Aye,' said uncle. 'It's bad oul stuff those sheets to be handlin'. So long now.'

Back inside, William said, 'Another cup of tea, John?'

'Well, I'll ...'

'No, not at all. You just sit there on your arse, let me. Here, and let me sugar it for you.'

He scraped a chair up beside me. I was scared but he had been warned so I tried to match his ways. Cupping his mug he flashed a hard look. I did likewise. He didn't like it and his eyes switched to the loaf of bread in front of me. His big fingers tugged and peeled off the hardened outer crust.

'So. You can give me all the lip you want to now, can't you?'

'No, I won't.'

'Well, not till you feel like it. That's about the size of it, isn't it? So you're off school for a week now?'

'Aunt Ruth says I can stay off longer if I want to.'

'Well, try and keep this place half decent. At least you can make the tea and tidy up. What's this crack about men on the stairs?'

'They were there, William. Honest to God, I saw them.'

'Did you now, by Christ? Well, I'm going for Violet,' and he was away.

Half an hour passed. As I washed the delft I wondered what Violet would think.

'Should you not be having a wee rest?' she said coming into the kitchen. 'Leave that, I'll do it.'

'I'm nearly finished.'

'Surely to Christ, Violet, he can wash the delft, except when there's a full moon,' joked William. Violet looked upset.

'William, don't,' she said and sat down beside me. 'You've had a turn. Well don't worry, you'll be alright. William says Aunt Ruth is getting you some tablets and you can stay off school until they come. No more robbing magpies' nests, and stay off the tractor.'

'I don't rob nests anymore.'

'Have you been begging bikes off Aunt Ruth?'

'No, honestly, she said she'd get them.'

She didn't look convinced. 'Have you eaten?' she asked.

'No.'

'I'll do you something. Go out to the car and bring me in them eggs.'

'Don't let him overdo it,' snapped William.

'Ah come on now, I'll do you some as well.'

After the feed I helped Violet wash the utensils and William went to McCune's to lay a hedge. Both brothers arrived home together late in the evening. Joe looked straight at me.

'So you're not in the best of form?'

Violet began to explain but he stopped her with a slanted gesture of his hand.

'I've heard it all from our fella here.'

'Ruth is looking for a word with you,' taunted William.

'We've had one. I bumped into her this afternoon in Markethill,' said Joe. 'There she was her very self, looking at bikes no less.'

'Well?'

'Well nothin'. She said her piece and I said mine, and that, as the man says, is that, and there'll be no more shootin' for you, boy. Well, you can use the air-rifle.'

'But the ·22's OK, Joe,' I pleaded.

'She's not. She'll shake your head.'

'There is no kick off the ·22 and I don't put her on my head, I'm not that stupid.'

'That's just the very thing I was talkin' about earlier,' said William. 'If Aunt Ruth could hear his cheek now she might understand a thing or two.'

On Saturday my aunt arrived with two brand-new Raleighs.

'There we go now, John and no racing handlebars, do you hear me?'

I nodded.

'And you and Violet must come and see us more. You have no excuse now. Where's the other two?'

'They're away at McCune's.'

'Has William touched you again?'

'No.'

'Well, if he does you ring me.'

143

'I will.'

'I've got to go now, John, I'm wanted at Mount Norris. We're having a Church dance. Do you want to come?'

I shook my head.

'You might win another rooster,' she laughed and hugged me. 'I'll see you Monday, with the tablets.'

Fifteen

❧

I dreamt my dream in long furry nights, flanked by a dim shape that slunk away from my searching eyes. Only when I was helplessly asleep would it let me look and then I wished it would go away forever on the vast acres of space my dream swept me through.

The strange thing up here is the cloud. There ought to be lots of them, but no, there is only one. Oval-shaped and whirling, it floats me away towards the dark edges of a yellow sky I can almost touch. What frightens me most is the giddy rushing through a flat spectrum, then the sharp dip into an endless valley of darkness.

'Please bring me back to the light,' a voice inside me begs.

Now I'm in the cold grey light of dawn. Our back yard is eerie; dusky shadows lurk by the edges of the stone piggeries. Green mould, like sour milk scum, lines the rim of the bucket handles. A lid is creeping over the sky but the light in the yard sharpens to an icy clearness, marking out the cold arena.

'They're coming, John, they're coming. Run for your life, son.'

'I'll make it to the house, Da, I will.'

'You won't. Get into the pig-house and lock the door. Quick. And the top part, son, they can jump through. Shove the bolt over.'

I lie against the damp stones. 'Get closer to the wall, son.'

'No, there's glass there. You mixed it with the cement when you concreted the floor to stop the rats gnawing

145

through.'

I'm lying still, hoping they cannot see me. I wonder which pig-house the others are in. I must be quiet now. They've arrived – six of them. I hear them howling, the swish of their long tails. I thought wolves would be ugly but they are so beautiful, so elegant. With fine-boned legs they stretch up the door, sniffing and whining. So majestic, so lithe. I wonder if the others are scared. The wolves are stalking around the square now. I can see the grey sheen of their sunken haunches. The big one is impatient. He lies down cocking his head like the lion they show at the start of the pictures. The badger-black patches of his thick coat look sharp as thistles. I'm sure he wouldn't hurt me, his face is sad.

When I awoke the light was flowing fast like a summer shower, and spangled columns of morning glittered on the wall. I flipped back the sheets and swung out my bony legs. The dust swirled then settled like pepper on the glinting mahogany wardrobe and I was giddy with joy at the morning's blueness. This was a new dream and persistent in its torture. I was beginning to wonder if it was the tablets. Perhaps they were having a quietening effect as Aunt Ruth said they would, but nobody had said anything about dreams like these.

I didn't know which sensation was worse, the rambling emptiness or the clogged cotton-wool denseness. Either way it was hard to concentrate. I think the teachers at school must have known. They were easy on me and I didn't have to do any homework for weeks. The answers were there but getting them out was impossible. I cared even less about school because I was so far behind. Somehow the alphabet had become a puzzle. I could reach 'O' then would have to stop and pick and stab.

In the fields winter was beginning to melt away. The sugar-coating on the ice was turning to a weak grey spawn. Patches of grass in bright bewildering green oozed and sucked and jigsaws of frost clustered on the window panes. I knew I would miss the quiet serenity of winter, the sharpness of icicles, the endless distance of dazzling fields. Snow-laden branches in thick hedgerows wept and dripped in the watery sunlight. I still carried my air-rifle but seldom used it, preferring to watch startled blackbirds sending sprays of powdery snow from the branches as they screeched their indignation.

How am I going to get out of here now? I wondered.

My stealth had been replaced by a slow-legged dreariness and if I was caught fumbling in William's pockets, I'd be joining the oul fella in Kilcluney. I yearned for my birthday and for Uncle Joe's arrival.

Spring blew quietly past me leaving a shy remembrance of peeping crocuses and graceful daffodils. They were all saying I had had another turn a few months back but it wasn't true. I was supposed to tell William when I was running out of tablets but when the tin was empty, seven days passed before I cracked on. It was good being my cheerful light-footed self again instead of stumbling around in a slow creeping mist. Later, I wished I hadn't told them about the dizziness. That's all it was, yet my head reeled like a spinning-top after I started back on the tablets. I clawed at the bark of a damson tree and slid down helplessly to the cool wet grass.

'I'll tell Ruth, she'll take you to see the doctor,' said William.

'It's because I've started back on the tablets,' I insisted.

'You shouldn't have run out. You've nothing else to think about.'

The doctor quizzed me and, scribbling noisily on his pad, said, 'This mustn't happen again, Mrs Hunter.'

'It won't. You have my word on it. I'll talk to Violet,' she promised.

No one believed it was just dizziness and they agreed that Violet would keep an eye on my tablets. In the car Aunt Ruth asked me again, 'Has he raised his hand to you, John?'

'No, honest he hasn't.'

The truth was, he had. It was slaps on the face now but I deserved it for cheeking him. I enjoyed it and picked my moments when others were there. Somehow I seemed to cry more although the slaps didn't hurt as much as the taunts.

'Look at him, he's got a lip that would trip a train,' William would sneer.

He too liked an audience but it backfired a couple of days after my fifteenth birthday. A kind of outrageous happiness had been trying to break through the weariness. In preparation for hay-cutting, we were clearing the shed of old bales. Winter seepage had caused those around the sides to turn black and mouldy, and the musky odour was stifling as bales slid from my hands like rotting pondweed.

'Jaysus,' William said, 'look at this corner, they're all shot.'

'It's no wonder, this shed isn't as good as the last one,' I replied and kicked at a loose galvanized sheet.

Like a turret on a tank he wheeled round, his eyes bulging, and blazed into me.

'The oul fella couldn't handle you, I can't and it doesn't look as if the tablets work either.'

Then in a trembling stoop he grabbed a bale, arched his back and flung. The binder twine snapped like a worn bootlace. Squares of compressed hay with white mildewed veins cart-wheeled into the yard.

In the kitchen, for our fry and mug of tea, William plopped the bacon on to my plate, stinging the back of my hand. After dinner we started work again joined by a neighbour, a large affable man called Geordie Deans. I decided to work harder but I knew by the scowl on William's face that he had not forgotten the incident.

'Right then, Lippy, what are you going to do now?'

'Fuck all if I can help it.'

The words spat from my mouth but my heart sank. I froze, then felt the bones in the back of his hand squash my lip into my mouth. Big Geordie's face reddened, and with a deep-throated chuckle he hurled a bale and William went sprawling. Picking himself up he laughed shakily, 'Cut the carry-on out,' and walked off to the byre. When he returned

148

five minutes later it was as if nothing had happened.

Most of my class said they were going to throw their bags over the hedge after the last day at school, but I had decided to hold onto mine; it was Molly's. It would be good to take it to England, then bring it back stuffed full of fivers.

I had been at it again, stealing. Three pounds this time, it couldn't be missed. William was flush. A Milk Marketing cheque on the Monday and two calves sold at Markethill the week before. I knew it was a lot of money but I had most of Saturday to think about it. Uncle Joe would be here in a month. It was time to start collecting my bits. Searching through William's wardrobe for an aerial photograph of the farm, his blue trousers felt heavy as I slid them across the wooden rail. With the back of my hand I clonked the change in his pocket, then inside there was a rustle and I pulled out a fistful of pounds and ten-shilling notes. I needed money for a suitcase and he was away hay-cutting at McCune's. I had been left to tidy the house. Several times I felt scared and put the money back, but he had kept my money so I decided to chance it.

When Cousin John arrived the next day with Aunt Ruth, I boasted and showed him the money. Catching his breath he shook his head, his face sour-milk white.

'By Jaysus, you're a better man than me, tell me no more,' he said.

Leaving school was a terrible anti-climax. Some did not turn up at all, others did not return after dinner. Our final lesson was reading but I just gazed out of the window as the sun beat down from a lazy sky. A sapling rocked in the gentle breeze which fanned the grass making it shake and tremble. At a quarter to four we wandered off aimlessly. A necessary chapter of our lives had ended. We were seasoned and armed.

I took my time dawdling home squinting at the heat-haze that shimmered above the white roads. After con-quering Finlay's Hill I lumbered along to the big oak tree, leaned my bicycle into the deep green of the hawthorns and stood like a scarecrow letting the breeze cool my skin. Above me the leaves chattered and I thought about leaving.

Patsy and I still enjoyed each other's company, but he knew I was not well and our mock fights in Marshall's fields had lost their mock ferocity. It annoyed me that he allowed me to win. I saw it as a warning for the future; how things would be if I stayed at home any longer.

'That's John Hughes over there,' they'd say.

'Where?'

'Him by the trailer. Poor bastard, hardly ever washes.'

'Ah sure now, it could've happened to anyone, who knows what God has in mind for us. Took a turn, a brave time ago but he's never been right since. They look after him they can. He doesn't do much, just makes the tea and fries the dinner. He's harmless really.'

I could see myself being like Harold Anderson. They'd find me an old house out of the way and come up for the crack when there was nothing else to do.

'Let's go and see yer man.'

'Ah leave the poor oul devil alone.'

'Come on, we're not going to harm him. We'll get 'im going just for the laugh.'

I wanted to tell Patsy my plans but was afraid that he might let it slip out. If Aunt Ruth found out she'd block me. How was I going to get the suitcase all the way from Markethill to Lisnagat, I wondered. Someone was bound to see me so it would have to be hidden somewhere.

Cutting hay at McCune's one day, William saw a rat nibble at a crust of bread. He went home for the shotgun. I thought it a waste just for one rat. He could have killed it with a stone but shooting had taken a hold on him. Just before going home later that evening I stood by a dried-up pond and watched a cluster of midges. Suddenly a hare bounded out of the grass, then slowed to a lollop along the headland.

'William,' I yelled, 'a hare, there's a hare.'

'Stick out yer lip and trip 'er,' he sneered and with a

chuckle turned to the others. 'Sure he couldn't miss 'er, could 'e?'

Someone managed a half-hearted laugh that faded quickly. Cousin John Hunter discarded the blade of grass he was whistling through. I looked into his simmering blue eyes and felt that he was thinking the same as me: If only I were big enough. We didn't speak, there was no need. I saw his eyes narrow as he watched William walk to the car.

I was angry with myself when I began to lose heart in my plans. What if Uncle Joe refused to take me without William's consent. He was still my guardian. I wondered if he would let me go if I asked him straight. If he said yes I would be home and dry, and if he said no I'd be no worse off. I decided to ask him that night. No, in the morning. No, Saturday night when he'd be in a good mood before going to town. It had to be done. Only two weeks left. A letter had arrived saying that Uncle Joe was coming in July.

On Saturday morning the sun was trying to break through a drizzle as I slid off for the cows. Seaboughan Lane was damp, the brown stones glistened and I breathed in the rich stench of the foliage. My courage was restored by the tranquillity and I heard myself saying, 'I'm going, I am.' An arrogant magpie cackled in defiance so I hurled a stone and listened to it bounce through the trees. Then I wavered back to uncertainty, at a loss about how to approach William.

'Can I go to England, William?'

'William, when Uncle Joe comes home can I go back to England with him?'

'William, how would it be if I tried a year with Uncle Joe?'

'What would be the chances of staying at Uncle Joe's for a year, William?'

Jaysus, which one was best?

At the river a heron lifted, flapped its wings lazily then banked out over the trees. The sun chased the drizzle away and a brilliant rainbow arched and sparkled over Seaboughan. When I entered the meadow a snipe burst from beneath my feet, my legs stiffening at its screech. I watched it skim away before diving into a swamp of rushes. The cows seemed glad to come home and filed calmly into the lane.

'Where have you been, boy? It's a good job I'm not in a hurry,' snapped William.

'Shall I wash their udders?'

'No, don't bother. Chain them up, then tidy the kitchen, it's a disgrace. I can't find anything in there.'

After I'd sorted out the kitchen I went into the byre and heard him singing. His head was resting on old Nancy's belly.

'Have you finished?' he asked in a soft voice.

'Aye, do you want anything else doing?'

'No, that's sound. You can go for a shot if you want, here's some pellets.'

He put the bucket down by the milk can and trickled pellets and chaff into my cupped hands. In the yard I regretted not asking him there and then. After an hour wandering around I stood at the flax-hole taking shots at corks bobbing in the black water. William took the cows back to Seaboughan. Perhaps after my afternoon of re-hearsals I could slip my question over in a nonchalant manner.

'What would be the chances of a person spending a year or so with Uncle Joe, William?'

I decided that was the one to go for but when the nerve-wrecking moment came in the scullery it all went wrong. Violet wasn't home yet and William was shaving. He slopped the stubby brush into the cracked mug, scurried it on the soap then lathered his face until it looked like the froth on a flooded river.

'You'll shine the toes of my shoes away, boy. Do the heels,' he remarked cheerfully.

Craning his neck he dragged the razor through the foam, puffing out his cheeks and shaving the lumps. After throwing water on his face he patted himself dry and looked for blood spots.

'Sound as a pound! Jaysus, what a fine-looking man! What do you think?' and he laughed my way.

My belly was in turmoil.

'Can I go to England?' I shouted in a rush. No more words would come.

'When were you thinking of?' he asked quietly, looking back in the mirror.

He didn't seem surprised. I sat still.

'Well, Uncle Joe will be here soon.'

'Do you think he'll have you?'

'Well, can I go if he will?'

'I suppose so.'

My heart threatened to burst through my chest and my stomach felt as if it had been twisted and wrung out to dry.

'Do you think you can do any good over there?' he asked, examining me in the mirror.

'Yes, yes. I'll work hard and make piles of money.'

'Can you behave yourself?' he demanded, spinning around.

'Honestly, I will.'

'Well, fair enough. We'll see what Uncle Joe says. He arrives the morrow.'

'I thought it was next Saturday.'

'No, Uncle John says it's the morrow.'

'I'm away now, William,' I squeaked and took to my heels before he could change his mind.

The evening light was fading fast as I approached the Goodfellows' cottage. Patsy came to the door munching a steaming soda farl, licking yellow butter from his craggy fingers.

'I can't come out, boy, I'm watching the wee ones.'

'I've something to tell you, Patsy.'

'What?'

'Guess.'

'How can I guess, it could be anything. Don't tell me you've got another pig.'

'It's better than that,' I grinned, shaking my head.

'Jaysus, boy, you haven't stolen a heifer, have you,' he

gasped, his eyes popping.

'I'm going away to England.'

'You're coddin' me on.'

'No I'm not, sure as I'm standing here I'm away to England with Uncle Joe.'

'You won't go.'

'I will.'

'You'll be back.'

'No I won't.'

'But you've got to get a job, John.'

'Anyone can find a job in England.'

'When are you away?'

'In two weeks.'

'What will William say?'

'He says I can go.'

'Can I believe it?'

'I'm tellin' you. Honest to God he said so.'

'What about Mrs Hunter?'

'I'm not telling her. Don't let it out, Patsy. She'll stop me if she hears tell of it.'

'Didn't you say she'd got you a start as a bricklayer?'

'I'm not going to be an oul bricklayer with hands cut to pieces in the winter. Have you found anything?'

'Nah, but I will.'

'Why don't you come as well?'

'What, me? To England? Nah, our Geordie says it's a fast life and the place is teeming with teddy boys. You can get knifed. A fella got himself kilt a while ago, down the town. Found him dead, they did, behind a church wall.'

'Ah away with yourself.'

'You ask Geordie, he'll tell you.'

'Well, I won't go down the town.'

Young Bernadette started to cry and Patsy had to go.

'Call up, boy, won't you?'

'Sure I'll be up before I go.'

'So long, John.'

As I climbed over the gate into the field I looked back at Patsy's cottage. I hadn't seen much of him these past few weeks. He was out most days looking for a job. As tall as William he was now; I'd only just noticed it. Even leaning at an angle against his door he was much bigger than me. I hadn't started shaving yet but at the door I had noticed a tiny piece of paper stuck to Patsy's red chin. He never said anything so I didn't let on, but we were such good friends I felt a little wounded. There was something tugging at my mind. It was hard to believe that William was letting me go.

Next morning Uncle John Hughes called. No one could have told him my news. He said that Uncle Joe had arrived and would be up to see us soon. Violet didn't want to talk about it.

'Sure you won't go, stop turning me grey before my time,' she said.

I went to church on my own on Sunday because I wanted a last look at Mammy and Da's grave. Rust had gathered on the identification plate of number 44. I felt as if I should say something special like the solemn prayer they said in the western films when homesteaders bury one of the posse in Indian country. I resented the feeling of stupidity within me as the idea echoed and laughed, so I whispered 'cheerio' and left.

Sixteen

ॐ

Every day I listened for the sound of cars along our lane, and a melancholy swarmed me when Uncle Joe didn't come. I decided to tell William that I was going for the suitcase anyway. I had three pounds two and ninepence. Pangs of guilt stabbed at me as I spun the mansion polish tin over the stone wall.

I walked towards Markethill thinking how quiet my life had become. England, England, I had become obsessed with the name. What would a big city be like? How far away would the countryside be? Did they laugh at the Irish? They were bound to call me Paddy.

A sudden shower turned to driving rain, battering my forehead until it pulsated. Near Finlay's Hill I sheltered beneath my big oak tree, watching a robin's feathers fluff and ripple as it clung to a barb of thorns. The wind ceased its vicious howling and I was away again with a stone for company. I kicked it all the way to Keady Street and never once did it touch the grass verge. Morgan's shop-window was a river of rain. I couldn't see any suitcases but there was a belt. I'd need one; I wouldn't want my trousers hanging round my arse. I'd have to see how far the money ran. The old fella who served Aunt Ruth surveyed me as I went in. I felt clumsy as his eyes stopped at my boots. The soles were hanging out like tongues.

'Yes, young Hughes. Is it boots you're huntin'?'

'No, a case.'

'What? A big case?'

'Aye.'

'Who's it for?'

'Me.'

I moved closer to the glass counter to hide my boots. My feet squelched and I felt hot and prickly.

'Why do you want a big case? What is going into it?'

'My things. I'm going away.'

'Where?'

'England,' I said proudly.

'England!' he exclaimed, 'you're a wee bit wee, wouldn't you say?'

'I'm fifteen,' I protested. 'I've left school.'

'If your Da was alive he wouldn't hear tell of it.'

'And I want a belt as well, a real one.'

'Are you meaning a leather one?'

'Well aye, but how cheap do they come?'

'Three and sixpence this one,' he said, swinging a silver-studded brown one before me.

'How much do the cases run?'

'Three pound two and sixpence.'

I was aware that my feet were beginning to smell.

'I'll come back for the belt,' I said.

'How much have you?'

I dug into my pocket and showed him the three crumpled pound notes and the two and ninepence. Clicking open the case he dropped the belt inside and took the three pounds. At the door he shook my hand.

'So long now. I still think you're a wee bit wee. Come and see us when you're home.'

'I will surely.'

As I pulled the door closed he stared after me and I caught the words, 'Holy Jaysus,' beneath his breath.

In the wet grey of the street I scooted, light-footed. Around the corner in Keady Street the wind could have sailed ships and I bowed my head, annoyed that the light case was threatening to part company with me. I tried holding it in front of me but it was hard work walking. Donelly's goats were startled by my appearance and skipped up the bank chewing their cud furiously. Old Tommy gave

157

me a knowing nod. I matched it and pushed on. When I was well past I looked back and he was still watching me.

I felt awkward clattering my way through the kitchen. William stared at the case.

'Holy Jaysus, are you taking half the house with you?' he asked, looking out the window as a car pulled into the yard. 'This is probably Uncle Joe now.'

Scrambling up the stairs I flung the case onto my bed then jumped down again, three steps at a time, bumping past William who was still standing by the window with a cup of tea.

'Slow down, you eejit, you nearly scalded me.'

I rushed out and wrenched open the door of Uncle Joe's car, shouting, 'Will you take me back to England, Uncle Joe? Will you?'

'Holy Jaysus, young John, let me out of the car first.'

'But will you?'

'What does your brother say?'

'He says I can go if you'll take me.'

'I'll take you, son,' he said and slapped his big hand on his knee.

Racing back to the kitchen I yelled at William, 'He says he will, he says he will.'

'Well, that settles that,' he said quietly and walked out to greet uncle.

After a few minutes of back-slapping we were all supping tea.

'Now what's this?' uncle said, turning to me. 'This fella wants to come to England. What do you think about it, Billy?'

'May as well if you can find a job to keep him out of trouble. He's no use to us.'

'Sure I can get him a start, in a factory.'

'So how's the crack out there,' William asked, switching the talk.

'Great country, great country altogether, William, it's a fine city, Coventry is.'

'Have you still the same job?' William enquired.

'Yes, and Nanny looks after the lodgers. The house is packed.'

'How is Aunt Anna?' I asked.

'Sound, son, sound. It will be a surprise for her to see you, John. You and our Cecil are the same age you know.'

'What about big Joe?' asked William. 'He was here a couple of years ago. He enjoyed the crack shooting at matchsticks in the yard.'

'Sure he's the finest young man in Coventry,' uncle boasted. 'Great job he has with the Admiralty.'

'What about Gougho?' asked William, topping up his mug.

'Oh he's fine. They're all fine. Each one of them's got a good job. Earning a fortune they are. Geordie Good-fellow's a bus-driver, the best there is. Sure there's jobs going beggin', William, and when you finish at four o'clock, that's it.'

William was shocked and so was I.

'There is none of this slaving till dark,' said uncle and explained about something called 'The Union'.

Joe roared into the yard on his bike. Uncle was pleased to see the nephew named after him. He enquired after his job, the farm, and told him how much he resembled his grandfather, and what a fine man he was.

'Are you sure it's alright to take John back?' asked uncle looking at my brothers.

'It's sound with me,' said Joe. 'Do you think you can make a man of 'im?'

'Sure you won't know 'im next time you see 'im,' laughed uncle.

'Have your case ready for Saturday, son.'

'Is that when we're leavin'?' I asked in surprise.

'Ay. The boat leaves at seven. I'll be here for you at four.'

'Christ, you're away early, boy!'

'Well, I want to go to Glasgow for a week to see your aunts. Come here, John, shake my hand. You're going to be a fine fella away from the farm now.'

'I'm away for cows,' I announced, wanting to be alone.

In Seaboughan Lane, elation and anxiety stormed me together. Where could I get money from? I was determined not to ask William. I'd ask Joe. If that failed I'd say nothing until we got to Belfast. Uncle wouldn't leave me behind.

Sitting on the river bank looking down into the black deep of the waters, I plopped in a small stone, watched my face dissolve and followed the ripples until they were no more. Being bad hadn't been bad for me. If I had been good I'd be staying here but because I was cheeky, unruly, useless round the farm and brought shame by stealing, I was free at last. I didn't blame William for not wanting me, but I knew he had his own reasons for letting me go.

Walking home in the rain with my suitcase, it had dawned on me that part of what I was leaving behind belonged to me. Father hadn't made a will and according to Aunt Ruth I was entitled to one-fifth of the farms. I realized that it was William's intention that I should have nothing, or at most, next to nothing.

'Lippy bastard. He's done fuck all to keep this place on its feet,' he'd say.

Molly had gone with a few hundred pounds settled on her and it would be the same for Violet, but Joe would be different; he'd worked hard and would not be put off. I felt certain that with me out of the way I wouldn't get much at all, but when I got on my feet I would come back to talk to William.

On Thursday morning I followed Joe to the shed and watched as he tried to start his motorbike.

'I'll give you a shove,' I offered.

Down past the chestnut tree the bike burst into life, white smoke trailing away into the July sunshine. My voice was lost against the roar of the machine. Easing off the throttle, my brother surveyed me with a questioning look.

'Will you give me the money for the boat, Joe?' I repeated.

With a wink and a grin he said, 'We'll see, boy, I'm late,' and he left me smothered in fumes. That meant yes with our Joe.

160

I found the aerial picture of the farm in the press with one of father taken three weeks before he died. There was one of Mammy in the front seat of the A40 and one of Violet with Molly on her wedding-day. I put them all in my case with my PT shorts, a pair of gutties, a white shirt, a navy pullover and some socks. I felt silly with that big case.

By Friday night Joe hadn't mentioned the money. Violet went to a dance with Billy and Joe went off to see Geordie Deans, so there was just William and me in the kitchen. The fast tick of the clock seemed deafening in the silence, interrupted by the odd question.

'Have you polished your shoes?'

'Yes.'

'What will you be wearing?'

'My school blazer.'

'Is your stuff in the case?'

'Ay.'

At last William said, 'I'm away to bed,' and was gone, leaving his wellingtons by the range. I flicked through the pages of Violet's *Ireland's Own*, then tuned the old wireless. It whined and crackled to Athlone and settled into jigs and reels. I turned up the volume for the hornpipes.

'Hey boy, turn that racket down. You should be in your bed anyway,' shouted William and the door slammed.

I awoke to a dull morning. The sky was blanket grey and a lone swallow sat heavily on the electric cable. William, up early, was scraping cold porridge from a saucepan.

'Do you want a cup of tay?' I asked as usual.

'No, I'll do it,' he said, grabbing the kettle. 'And you don't have to go for the cows.'

'I don't mind, William. There's plenty of time.'

Going back upstairs for my jumper I met Joe trotting down. 'Is the tay on, boy?'

'Yes, William's done it.'

Opening the case I looked at my belongings, snapped it shut and sat on the bed. The leather belt was much too long. I'd have to make another hole in it. As I measured it round me the door swung open.

'I've got to go, boy,' said Joe and a brown envelope skimmed across the room. 'There's your fare, John, now you do well for yourself, won't you?'

'I will, Joe.'

'I'll be hearing after you,' and raising his hand he wheeled quickly away.

I picked up the envelope. It was his wages still sealed with eight pounds inside. Joy flooded through me. Back in the kitchen, bursting to go for the cows, I was stopped by Violet.

'I'm late, John, will you make me a drop of tay?' she asked as she raked a comb through her tangled hair. 'Do you think you'll go?'

'I'm going.'

Cupping her mug with both hands she blew gently on the tea, gave up and plopped in more milk.

'I hope I'll see you when I come home,' she said.

'You won't. I'll be away.'

'You will write to me, won't you?'

I nodded as she whispered goodbye and ran out the door. Following her to the yard I watched as she grabbed her bike from the shed. At the corner she waved.

Seaboughan Lane was quiet. A fieldfare skipped across, warbled and hovered against the sky. The cows were lazy so I urged them along. At the fairy tree I stood under for one last look. For a week I had intended to do this and I didn't feel silly, no one could hear as I said goodbye to the trees, the hedgerows and the swamp of mud. I tiptoed through each day. I knew I would miss my lane but I had to go.

'Get a move on,' I shouted and cracked the behind of a young heifer.

At dinner-time belly-pains and excitement made it hard to eat but it could be a long time before I got another feed.

'Here, do you want this?' said William, giving me a sausage that would choke a dog.

At four o'clock he caught me glancing at the clock for the fifth time in as many minutes.

'He should be here any minute. Mind you behave out

there and when you get a job send us what you can. Here's the man 'imself now.'

My heart pounded as Uncle Joe stepped out of a small black car. Struggling into my blazer I stood by my case.

'You're ready then,' he said with a grin.

'He is. Since two o'clock,' said William.

I hope he doesn't want tea, I want to go, I thought.

'Uncle Joe, can I drop up to say cheerio to Patsy?'

'Well by Christ, we can't be all day, son, it's a brave oul drive. And don't worry, Billy,' he said, slapping my brother's back.

'He'll do well.'

'Sure you'll have a mug of tay before you go?'

'No, Billy. I wouldn't mind seeing Mrs Goodfellow myself.'

Grabbing my case I went first. Uncle put it in the back of the car then squeezed my brother's hand and told him he'd see him next year.

'Sound, sound. Make sure he gets a job.'

'He will, I'll see to that myself.'

'So long, Uncle Joe.'

'Cheerio, Billy.'

'So long, John.'

'Cheerio, feed Spot, won't you?'

'Ay, when he's here.'

At the cottage Mrs Goodfellow answered the door.

'It's only a quick call, Cassie, John wants to say cheerio.'

Francy was sitting in his usual chair by the range, puffing his pipe. Standing up he shook uncle's hand then mine.

'By Jaysus, you must be doing well, Joe, you're looking younger each year. So you're takin' this fella with you?'

'I am that.'

'You'll look after him, Joe, won't you?'

'Don't worry, Francy, he's in good hands.'

Mrs Goodfellow wrung her handkerchief. 'Cheerio, John,' she sniffed in my ear as she hugged me. 'No, Joe, I can't take that,' she said, trying to hand back a five-pound note.

'Go on, you're a sound woman and I want you to have it,' insisted uncle.

'Jaysus, you're a terrible man, Joe Hughes,' she laughed, and clutching the money she turned to me. 'You will come home and see us, John, won't you?'

'Sure he'll be back next year.' Uncle buttoned his coat and went outside.

'Cheerio, Francy.'

'Cheerio, young Hughes,' he smiled, taking off his cap and scratching his head. Patsy was grinning sheepishly. 'Leave it there, boy,' he said, holding out his hand. 'You won't stick it.'

'I will.'

'Good luck to you, John,' they said and followed me to the door. I could see Patsy's smile dissolve to despondency as I returned their waves.

Uncle talked all the way to the docks. From Lisnagat to Portadown, almost every farmhouse got a mention: 'Cow bulled there'; 'Sow boared here'; 'I'm banned out of that pub'; 'Kicked the shite out of two bad boys at this one.'

This was my dream come true. From the age of twelve I had wanted independence and now I wanted to be famous too. Perhaps I'd become a pop star.

'Have you gone deaf, son? That's Lisburn on the right. So, as I was saying, then the next two bastards ...'

'Which two?'

'Are you not listening? Like I was sayin', there I was standing in the corner, like the decent man I am, with a drop of porter, when in these boys came and started throwin' their weight about. You'd have thought they owned the fuckin' place. They'd eyed me up and began laughing. The wee one came first, they always do, so I give 'im a scelp with the back of me hand and he started slobberin'. Then this big ginger bastard said, "Do ya fancy yer chances, Paddy?" The wastrel, I've thrown better men out of the corn field. "Joe Hughes knows his chances," I told 'im. He didn't go down with the first but he did with the second, then before I knew where I was another hure

164

landed on me back like a cat. Well by Jaysus then the going really got rough. A big gypsy built like a haystack broke a bottle so I hit him with a table and he split open like a cut pig. None of the other cowards in there would lend a hand, shower of snivellin' bastards hid in a corner. D'ya hear me, John?'

'Yes. What happened then?'

'They took to their heels and ran out of the door like dogs. If only my lad Joe had've been there, he's got a back like a lion.'

'Where did you say Lisburn was, Uncle Joe?'

'Miles back, sure we're nearly here. Why?'

'Just thinking.'

'Thinking what?'

'Just how near we are to Belfast.'

'Have you been here before, John?'

'Only once. Aunt Ruth brought me for a day out.'

'Fine woman, your Aunt Ruth. Did you tell her you were leavin'?'

'Sure, I did.'

'That's sound. I didn't have the time to see her.'

He stopped the car. 'This is it, John. Catch a hold of them two cases and stay by the car whilst I hand these keys in,' he said.

A crimson sun the size of ten moons slipped behind a maze of cranes and an unfamiliar breeze wafted the smell of a thousand rotting cabbages.

'What way now, uncle?'

'You stick with me, John, there's some bad boys around here, they'd take the shirt off yer back.'

I felt a little scared. There were so many people milling and jostling and Uncle Joe walked so quickly. Trying to stick to him I trod on the back of his heel a few times but he didn't notice and surged on.

'There she is, Uncle Joe, there she is,' I shouted as the gleaming white boat appeared. I couldn't believe its size. He grinned at me.

'You've never seen the likes of that before, have you?'

'No. It's bigger than our hayshed. Are we getting on now?' I asked.

'No, hold your horses,' and stopping at a window he asked for two tickets. 'One adult and one child,' he said, pointing back at me, 'and a berth apiece while you're at it.'

'What's that?' I asked.

'A bed, John, it's a long rough crossing.'

'I can't have one.'

'Why can't you?'

'I've only got my boat fare,' I lied, handing him a five-pound note.

'That'll do sound.'

'Does the child want a berth or not, sir?'

'Yes, two of us together.'

The man grinned at me and I felt stupid. 'Bet he thinks I'm a right eejit,' I thought.

People were queuing on the harbour's edge and the gangplank was packed.

'Give me the cases, John,' said uncle, throwing out his chest and marching forward.

'There's a queue,' I whispered.

'Queue?' he shouted. 'Your uncle's never queued in his life and he's not starting now.'

Running up the gangplank my big case bumped and knocked against people. Looking over his shoulder uncle bellowed, 'Stay with me.'

I felt nervous because they were all raring up, shouting, 'Hey boy, there's a queue here.'

At the entrance we were tackled by a uniformed man.

'There's a queue down there and it's for standing in.'

'Get out the friggin' way, Joe Hughes is boardin' this ship.' The man staggered back. Bowing my head I followed in.

'Over there, John,' uncle said, pointing his suitcase at a wooden seat in the centre of the deck. 'Good seat, this is, near the bar and we can keep our eyes on this shower of thieves.'

Watching the scramble I was mesmerized by the crowd.

Big men, little men, battered cases, fat women and scrawny women clutching bags and tethered by clatters of children crying, shoving and pushing.

'Watch him,' warned uncle. 'Don't like the look of that one. Jaysus, look at this one.'

The hoot of the boat made me jump.

'We're away, John, we're away,' he said, slapping my knee. 'Would you like somethin' to eat?'

I didn't get a chance to reply.

'Mind them cases,' he commanded and disappeared into the crowd. Suddenly I was gripped by fear. He was gone and I was worried about the cases. Sandwiching them together between my knees I stared at the floor. A man took uncle's seat.

Don't look up, I told myself, willing Uncle Joe to come back. Brown shoes and green trouser-bottoms appeared in front of me. It was him, a plate in either hand, signalling to the man to move.

'You're the boy that jumped the queue, aren't you?' the man said accusingly.

'I am,' said uncle, frowning menacingly at the stranger. 'Tell me,' he continued, bending forward with the plates and shifting his feet for balance as the boat rocked, 'have you booked yourself a berth for tonight?'

'I have and what about it?' challenged the man.

'Well, if you don't get out of my seat you won't be needin' it, you'll be fuckin' swimming back to Belfast.'

The stranger picked up his case and disappeared. 'I told you, John, they're a bad load of hures on this boat.'

The fry would have fed six farmers but I was starving and even ate a sausage that Uncle Joe didn't want.

'Go upstairs, John, and you'll see the harbour, I'll mind the cases,' he said when we had finished.

He sensed my reluctance. 'Go on, no harm'll come to you while I'm here.'

It was cold on top and the wind battered my face. I've made it. It's hard to believe but it's true, I thought. I wondered what Violet was doing? William would have taken the cows down Seaboughan Lane by now.

The light was fading and in the distance a veil of grey rain softened the land.

'It's cold up there, Uncle Joe,' I said, sitting down beside him a few minutes later.

'Ay, but the bar's open. What you havin'?'

'An orange, please.'

'You're not drinking orange. Have a whiskey, it'll warm you up. If yer man comes back shout me and I'll cleave his head off.'

The whiskey seared warmth into my belly.

'You'll have another one, John?' and he was away again.

'I feel a wee bit light in the head, Uncle Joe,' I confessed after my second drink.

'Well, we'll be away to our beds then.'

We were shown our berths by a lad not much older than me and uncle gave him ten shillings.

'Have the top berth, John. You've never been in one of them, have you?'

'It won't fall, will it?'

'No,' he laughed and gave me a shunt up. 'Are you keeping your shirt on?'

'Yes, I'm a wee bit cold.'

'Right, well go straight to sleep and when you wake up we'll be at Heysham.'

Turning to the wall I closed my eyes. All I had to do was sleep and I would have made it.

'John?'

'Yes?'

'Get out of bed and lock that door. The place is full of hures and gravediggers.'

Seventeen

When we arrived in England I realized that I was following in the footsteps of many Irish people who had left home through strife and poverty, in search of a better life. How tough things could be was first explained to me by Jimmy Greenaway, a lodger at my uncle's house. He was an old bent man with a productive cough and a face like a fist. He had left home in the mid-'fifties and sheltered in Irish guesthouses, the only refuge available then to the increasing number of exiles. He told me that the 'Paddies' were not liked and were classed as thick navvies, and described how difficult it was to obtain credit and find work or a place to live. With tears in his eyes he relived the days he had to fight his way up Spon Street because of his nationality. His statement was chilling but it did not affect me. I was here now and determined to succeed. My exploration of the locality was as fascinating as my childhood discovery of snow. People, shops, houses, buses, cars and pets, all standing, running, moving, working, and so greatly different to anything I had ever seen. On street corners juke-boxes in steamy cafés blasted out Joe Brown's great hit, 'A Picture of You'.

My uncle's terraced house was crammed with Irish men. Cousin Joe and I shared a room with George and Fran Goodfellow and Gougho. Everyone welcomed me but repeatedly warned me with an air of experienced superiority that this was not rural Ireland. I realized that my cousins were no longer country folk but sharp streetwise kids able to side-step lanky teddy boys in drainpipe trousers with boot-

169

lace ties as long as their sinister sideburns. Uncle gave me a week to find a job, during which my board was free. I did not tell anyone that I was ill because I was afraid of being sent home. A job, or 'the start' as we called it, was vital, a guarantee of security.

'Garage Attendant Wanted', said the advert in the local newspaper.

'What's a garage attendant?' I asked Cousin Joe.

'It probably means working the petrol-pumps, John.'

It seemed a great chance to me. I could write to Violet and say that I was training to be a mechanic. My illusion was short-lived.

'You're just the man for the job, Paddy, thirty shillings a week but you must keep the place clean,' the foreman said.

Sweeping floors was far removed from my fantasies but I had the start and agreed to give Aunt Anna one pound per week. In an attempt to boost my finances, I joined in the Friday evening game of cards at Uncle Joe's. My skill did not equal my ability at pitch-and-toss, and after ten minutes I was relieved of ten shillings.

On several occasions Cousin Joe sensed my distress and provided me with bus fares for work. At the garage my prowess as floor-sweeper greatly impressed the foreman and soon I was promoted to petrol-pump attendant. I was trained by a big-bellied man whose ambitions, like mine, ran ahead of his ability.

'Right, son, I'm forecourt supervisor, going on foreman. If it's cash it goes in there, but credit customers sign here, got it?' Embarrassed at not knowing what credit meant, I replied yes. I was given oversized brown overalls to wear and cheekily chirped out, 'Cash or Credit, Sir?' as customers drove in.

All went well until one day a city boy in a red sports car flashed into the forecourt and requested credit for a tankful of petrol. After he drove off I discovered he had given me a false name and registration number. My dreams of being a mechanic ended abruptly as the foreman handed me my cards, wished me luck, and said, 'McAlpine's are taking on labourers.'

Uncle Joe was furious and bellowed at me to find another job quickly as Aunt Anna could not afford to keep me. He was not the friendly giant who had patted my head in Ireland, but a much-changed man given to aggressive moods. The image he had portrayed of a happy successful city-dweller was a myth; his heart lay far away in the corn fields of Ireland. We were all wary of him on his return from the pub and attempted to humour him, but only Cousin Joe with his strength and reasoning could do so.

Late one night, having hounded Aunt Anna from her bed to cook him his favourite fry, uncle warned a lodger to stop his continuous singing of the last two lines of Chuck Berry's popular song, 'No particular place to go'. The joker proceeded to goad him with quite a good impression of the pop star. I thought my uncle had relented when he disappeared from the room, but two minutes later he thundered back flinging a packed case at the man. 'Get out of here, you hure,' he roared.

At the dark narrow exit uncle planted his large boot on the backside of the lodger and bawled, 'Now you've got no fucking particular place to go.'

Sometimes he was very generous and any money won on the horses was unbegrudgingly used to treat us. His ability to string together good priced horses in multiple bets was uncanny. One Saturday afternoon, as uncle's sixth horse of the day romped home a winner, rough calculations revealed that he had won several hundreds of pounds. He rushed off to Jimmy Clithero's dimly lit betting office, crowded with disappointed down-at-heel punters, and slapped his ticket down onto the counter.

'Pay up,' he shouted.

The elfin-like proprietor with two wooden legs, nick-named the 'Clithero Kid' after his champion greyhound, pointed to the three hundred pound pay-out limit.

'That's the most I have to pay you, Paddy, we have a limit here,' he insisted.

Uncle drew back his broad shoulders, thrust out his

massive chest and roared, 'Limit, no one puts a limit on Joe Hughes,' and in a raging temper smashed up most of the shop. Eventually, in sheer desperation, the kid threw him a bundle of notes.

My next job as a butcher's boy lasted only a month. I inflicted more cuts on my fingers in those few weeks than there were chops in the window. Working in an ice-cold room at the back of the shop, I was always relieved to get out into the sun for lunch, which I bought at the hot food bar across the road. I became addicted to the savoury steak-and-kidney pies, consuming several each day. I was not sorry to leave that job, but I missed my walks home through the busy city centre; the motorized sweepers brushed up the day's debris and paper-sellers bawled 'Evening Telegraph', or 'Pink and a White', each with his own special shout as if to claim that his *Telegraph* was best.

Three more unhappy months were spent on smoke-filled buses travelling to the other side of town to work in yet another butcher's shop. Now I looked so down at heel, I suffered the indignity of being banished to the rear of the premises to make sausages. The proprietor's wife, a plump dark-haired woman, took pity on me and fed me sandwiches. However, she caused Aunt Anna considerable distress when she rang complaining that my clothes were unfit to be worn in the shop. My aunt explained that it was difficult enough to care for her own six children, never mind feed and clothe another on one pound per week. Even the fashionably dressed dummies staring out of shop-windows seemed to sneer at my scruffy appearance.

As I travelled home that Christmas evening in 1962, giant snowflakes clung to the windows of the bus where I sat clutching my National Insurance Cards and eating the large pork pie that I had been given along with the sack. I was to spend Christmas with Aunt Minnie, one of father's sisters, who lived in what was known as a desirable part of the city. I had visited her many times and liked this warm-hearted woman with a strong Scots accent. She had left her native Ireland as a young woman and settled in Glasgow with her two sisters, Annie and Priscilla. Lack of work brought her entire family to Coventry but apart from her accent you could be forgiven for thinking that she had lived all her life in this sprawling city. Sparkling eyes and the smile of a motherly landlady greeted me as I stood empty-handed on her doorstep on Christmas morning.

This was Christmas as never before. A family eating, laughing, talking, exchanging presents and united in affection. Each of my new cousins, Billy, Shirley and Hazel, had bought me a small gift. Aunt and Uncle David delighted me with a new shirt. I sat sheepishly on a leather chair and caught sight of myself in the sideboard mirror, my school blazer worn and frayed, my face unsmiling beneath a ruffle of black wavy hair. I thanked them for the presents, swallowing the fierce anger that rose from my belly and swelled into my face. This anger was to become an occupant within me and inexorably shape my life.

Being a young Irishman with no qualifications, an unkempt appearance and a poor record of employment I found it hard to get work. Aunt Anna kept me as well as her finances would allow and now I visited Aunt Minnie more often to eat piping hot Scottish dinners.

In the late spring of 1963, Aunt Minnie invited me to live at her house because she knew that life at Uncle Joe's was difficult. I was overwhelmed by her kindness. The offer instilled a bold confidence in me, rather as if I were backing a horse in the knowledge that if it lost I would get my money back. A few days later I repaid my uncle's kindness by stealing two blankets off my bed, packed my case and left.

I am still not certain why I didn't go straight to Aunt Minnie's. Perhaps I wanted to be alone, determined to gain success and independence purely on merit. For whatever reason, that night I stood on the concrete walkway of a breezy park and looked across to the winking lights of the city. The two weeks I spent living there, sleeping on a wooden bench wrapped in my stolen blankets, held no fear for me other than my being terrified of Aunt Minnie finding out. Her generosity was balanced with a firmness which demanded respect. Hygiene took priority in her house, and I am sure that the idea of her nephew living rough would have loosened the temper which simmered in her laughing blue eyes.

Besides trying to find work I still visited her three times a week, necessitating a visit to the local slipper-baths to make myself presentable. This turned out very well as the old man who ran the council wash-rooms took a liking to me. Most of the time he kept my case, which allowed me the freedom to search for work and food. I told him that if I had a tin-opener I could provide for myself. He rummaged in his locker, handed me one and with a grave expression said, 'Don't get caught, son.'

The best food was the easiest to steal, tins of John West salmon fitted easily into my blazer pocket. I picked my shops carefully, preferring those run by older people, as they seemed less suspicious. In Broadgate, the centre of Coventry, with its Lady Godiva statue and fiendish Peeping Tom, I felt capable of stealing anything, even one of the large red buses that shuddered in the morning sunlight, but it was the haunt of the bus's custodians I was more interested in. Drivers and clippies, engrossed in conversation, invariably did not have time to finish their breakfasts before an inspector signalled with a glance at his watch that it was time to go. Here I devoured sausages, eggs, bacon, toast, anything that was left behind. The anger within lay quiet during these survival expeditions, appeased by a sharpened cunning and an ability to shuffle from plate to plate like a bee visiting flowers. At night in the park if I could not sleep, I watched the lights and pretended that one was blinking especially for me.

One bright morning I was startled by a fast chattering sound and was astounded to see a small fluffy animal, not unlike a rat, sitting on my bench swishing its tail. Unperturbed by my presence, it reared onto its hind legs and nibbled at something held in its front paws. I had never seen a squirrel before and thought perhaps the local zoo had lost one of its inhabitants. Somehow the curiosity of the squirrel prompted me to look at myself. Here I was, not too well, with just two blankets and a bushy-tailed rat for company.

The following Sunday Aunt Minnie gave me one of her long angry looks, a kind of disgusted appraisal as if to question what had become of me. She insisted that I had a bath while she washed my clothes. Again she offered me a home and this time I gratefully accepted and promised to move the following day. My cousin Billy often got together with Uncle Joe for verbal sparring sessions, so it would only have been a matter of time before he realized I had already absconded. I was nervous when he offered to collect me in his car and relieved when Aunt Minnie advised me to make my own way, thus eliminating any possibility of ill feeling between the two families.

Inspired by having a home, I soon had a new job. The first car wash had appeared in a city-centre car-park, called the 'Five Minute Car Wash'. Lads like myself were paid two pounds per week to don green waterproofs and scrub cars in cold water while their business owners sat back puffing cigars. Working conditions were miserable, but with so many youngsters desperate to earn money, it was a case of take it or leave it. After two weeks, my body numb with cold, I left, furious that the foreman would not pay me my final week's wages.

When I got home Billy listened to my sad tale, then pulled on his big boots and drove me to town. The foreman nervously tried to bundle his takings into a briefcase when Billy flung open the door.

'Yes, Sir, what can I do for you?' he asked shakily.

'It's not what you can do for me, Jimmy, it's the wee lad here, pay him his money.'

'Don't get mad, get even,' said Billy with a wink as I stuffed four pound notes into my pocket.

I spent the next five years working in a factory making radiators. It was often lonely and depressing, but not without its moments of happiness and opportunity. The air was filled with the noise of heavy machinery and the pungent smell of the soapsuds used to cool metal. The grey-faced drudges, swinging hand-presses or stamping the pedal of spot-welders in the poorly lit, greasy environment, seemed to have accepted a terrible sentence for the chance to earn good money. However, good money it was, and I was able to improve on the one pound per week contribution for my keep. I paid three pounds, and enjoyed a manly feeling of independence.

Increased wealth brought about a subtle change of attitude. I attended the local Methodist church for a year, secretly admiring a girl called Annette, who always gave me a knowing but guilty look as we left church. When I finally found the courage to ask her out she replied, 'When were you thinking of?'

I was delighted and my confidence soared. Already I had heaped vengeance on the mocking shop-dummies in town and purchased new clothes. Feeling wonderfully spiteful, I managed to acquire a blue pullover that had graced one of the simpering charlatans. For my first date I wore a new black blazer, grey trousers, and winkle-picker shoes.

Annette, a plump blonde with a beehive hairstyle, lived in a tree-lined road in our neighbourhood. Her father, an elderly balding man with screeches of white hair combed back over his head, bore more of a resemblance to a Gestapo chief than a senior churchman as he surveyed me at the door.

'So, you have called upon Annette, have you?'

'Yes.'

'Well, you had better come in.'

In a deep green lounge, Annette was waiting in an armchair. Her father positioned himself at such an angle that he did not need to move his head to monitor our embarrassed glances. She talked of having just seen the Beatles at Coventry Hippodrome and demonstrated how exciting they were by raking her fingernails roughly through her stiff set hair. Later on, her mother, who never spoke, served us tea in delicate rose cups that chinked and rattled on fine saucers. At ten o'clock, her father stood up and announced it was bedtime. Annette remained seated while he led me to the door and grunted 'Goodnight.'

The following Sunday I waited on a corner where I knew she would pass and asked her for an explanation. She told me firmly that her father did not approve of the Irish and that we would not be meeting again.

In the early spring of 1964, I decided to join Stoke Ex-Servicemen's Boxing Club, convinced that the capacity to deliver a good right hand in this city of wide boys would be helpful. Two bus-rides were necessary to reach the old converted house used mainly as a drinking den for those who had served in the war. The wooden gymnasium floor was bleached white by years of sweat, skipping and fast footwork from aspiring champions. The trainer, a flat-faced cockney with a spreading nose, said that my action reminded him of a windmill. He worked on my style and fitness for months until I was able to take part in Sunday morning sparring sessions watched by a huddle of foot-shuffling old men clutching pints of beer. After our skirmishes we sat in the brown peeling hallway, eating crisps and drinking lemonade that stung our bruised lips.

My earnings at the factory rose with the introduction of piece-work, a method of payment where workers were rewarded according to the quantity they produced. My job was to remove paint that had lodged in screw-holes of radiator brackets. The repetitive work could be monotonous and mind-destroying, but I used the time to dream of ways to improve myself – ways towards independence, success and financial security.

I continued with the Mysoline tablets as prescribed. The side-effects were as severe as ever. Most of the time drowsiness swam around my head like a hangover that would not go away. Learning to cope with this alien was not easy but worst of all was the feeling of stupidity and the inability to absorb or retain information or even to remember simple messages.

Walking at dusk provided me with a sense of purpose;

anyone walking at this hour seemed to have purpose. My uncle David started night-shift at 9.30 in a local factory so I used to accompany him there every evening and enjoyed our chats as we breathed in the sharp night air. A small tank of a man, he marched like a soldier through the yellow-lit streets. This marching had become an established routine from my early visits to his house when he used to escort me home to Uncle Joe's. After bidding him goodnight, I would return to Spencer Park and roam the perimeter until the trees disappeared into the night. If no one was around I did exercises to disperse the strange core of energy that burned in my belly. Sometimes this energy forced me to double up in agony with stomach cramp.

In pensive moments, I slipped back to Ireland. Most of my thoughts concerned Violet, who maintained a steady flow of letters, always carrying the same advice, to be thrifty and save money. One day Aunt Minnie showed me a letter she had received from Violet thanking her for taking me into her home. It ended on a note that stunned me, lowering my fragile self-esteem.

'Take care of wee John, he is a bit simple and chicken-hearted.'

I do not think the letter was meant to be hurtful, but in a single line my sister expressed the family's general opinion of me. I thought about what would have happened had I stayed in Ireland. Thankful that I had avoided the fate of being treated like a simple idiot and shut away in a lonely farmhouse, my spirits lifted a little. My aunt was as disgusted by this letter as she had been by the one I had received from William some months earlier, asking for money. A few weeks later I was amazed to receive another letter from him inviting me to come home.

'We have things to talk about,' he wrote, 'if you can read between the lines.'

Aunt Minnie, aware of all that had gone before, pleaded with me not to go.

'John, I can tell you from experience, once you have left there is no going back,' she warned.

However, even her threat of not allowing me to live at her house anymore could not deter a force stronger than my own reasoning. So I returned with trepidation, and William's initial welcome was pleasing.

Joe was in hospital having a small operation and Violet was out at work all day, so William and I were alone. After three nights he called me into his bedroom and asked bluntly how much I would settle for.

'Whatever my rightful share is,' I replied.

The moment I spoke I wished I was back in England. I will never forget what followed. For several minutes I endured a ferocious battering beyond anything I had ever encountered. This time he concentrated mainly on my body. I believe to this day I saved my life by not fighting back because he stopped only when I lay on the floor whimpering. Dazed and confused I was pushed into the car and at the end of the lane he stopped and asked if I would like some more. I shook my head speechlessly. He cursed me as he aimed the car along the country lanes. At my sister Molly's house he pushed me out and flung my case after me. His parting words, 'Never come home again,' still echo through the caverns of my mind.

After knocking loudly on Molly's door, I waited to give her time to get dressed. It was midnight. Stepping back I looked up at the bedroom window and was pleased to see Molly peering down. I continued to wait and after a few minutes anxiously knocked again. There was no reply and I looked back at the window. The curtains were closed. I stood in the cold dark of the yard and felt something leave me, something important that I knew might never return. The last shackles had been cut. I was free.

I knew where I could seek refuge for the night and, as I walked the black half-mile to our postman's house, I vowed to fight for my share of the farms.

I had only ever seen George Gardner in his uniform and the sight of the whiskered giant wrapped in white night attire made me laugh inwardly. When I explained my predicament he shook his head and hastily made up a bed on the sofa muttering, 'Brothers should not fight.' I couldn't sleep and listened to George's one hundred clocks chime and cuckoo through the night, punctuating my thoughts. Now I had the justification to fight and the motivation to work hard so I could pay a solicitor to claim what was mine.

The next morning as I bid George goodbye, I told him why I could never come home again. His reply warmed me: 'Nonsense, you're Willie Hughes's youngest son and you can always stay with me.'

Now I clearly understood the reasons for Aunt Minnie's anxiety. It would be wrong to say that the visit left me in a state of mental ruin but I knew there was a strong probability that William would turn the rest of the family against me, especially Violet. When her letters dried up my fears were confirmed and I knew that the sooner I fully accepted I was alone and eradicated Ireland and family from my thoughts, the sooner I could plot a path to success.

The powerful energy that roamed my body and played a major role in my survival challenged the drowsy mind, often injecting an exuberance into my veins which made almost anything possible. Other times it lay quiet and left me to bumble along.

While money was a strong consideration I thought it best to look to the future and tried to envisage what my life would be like in twenty years' time. I did not want to end up as a vacant-faced machine operator and the foreman was pleased when I decided to attend night-school to study mechanical engineering. I found retention of information difficult but after twelve months scraped through my exams.

At the boxing club the trainer had coaxed my style from a wild wading eagerness to a tight defensive crouch. My favourite punches were a fast left jab followed on by a right cross. I soon had my first bout and was delighted to travel to Birmingham for the finals of the Midland Counties ABA Championship. Billy said I should tell the trainer that I was receiving treatment for epilepsy. After his initial disappointment he informed me that the Club was prepared to pay for a private medical report. Hatton Hospital, ten miles outside Coventry, was a home for the mentally deranged. On a grey damp morning I alighted from the bus and watched the tall red building loom out of the mist. I walked along the pathway until I spotted the three stark letters, EEG. The test was completed in silence and I was on my way home within an hour. Three weeks later my trainer solemnly explained that my boxing career was over.

'They could find nothing wrong, John, but have advised us not to take the chance. I am sorry, son, you have a good right hand, and you would have won more fights than you would have lost.'

In a desperate bid to hold onto my aspirations, I joined another club under the name of John O'Brien. Edgewick Trades Hall Amateur Boxing Club was renowned for its champions. The trainer asked if I had boxed before and was suspicious when I said I had not. One evening he asked me to do some sparring. My partner was reigning Midland Counties Champion and I was truly out of my class against the wiry hard-boned lad. At the end of round two, an old Irishman, watching the one-sided affair, came up and whispered in my ear, 'Is there many more like you back home?', explaining that the other lad was a Southpaw and because of the contrasting styles I could not reach him with my left. In round three, I followed the old man's advice, and flashed across a right hand that landed spot on the chin.

'Very clever, Paddy,' seethed the trainer as he helped my opponent to his feet. 'Now which club have you previously boxed for?'

The game was up and I made a full confession. I was offered the chance to train but still couldn't take part in the sport I enjoyed so much, all because of my medical history.

Eighteen

✺

The Beatles' unique sound saturated Coventry's music shops and they did a roaring trade selling records, music sheets and guitars on credit, to youngsters wishing to emulate the Fab Four. For me, though, no one could equal 'The King' – Elvis Presley. A picture of him clad in black leather astride a motorcycle and looking mean influenced me to purchase a motorbike on the hire purchase, and soon I was tearing around Coventry on a red BSA C15. To complete the image I bought a leather jacket, black jeans, flying boots and a white silk scarf. Riding alone became boring, and after a while I ventured into La Ronde, a greasy café on the main thoroughfare. I rode with its motley gang for six months. They were unkempt and revelled in their scruffiness; when not airing their knowledge of bearings and crankcases they exhibited their skills as pin-ball wizards on the gaming machines. Nonetheless, they were a friendly lot, offering advice on how to soup up engines. After a few weeks I was amazed to see a lot of the riders' L-plates disappear and felt envious as they flashed full licences in corners as though they were holding an ace hand of cards.

'Have you put in for your test, Irish John?' asked a tall thin bespectacled lad with a striking resemblance to Buddy Holly.

'Not yet,' I replied, pleased that someone was interested.

'Well, when you do I'll take it for you. It will cost you a deep sea diver.'

Coventry's youths had now clearly split themselves into

two groups, Mods and Rockers. The Mods rode flashy, psychedelic scooters decorated with badges. Most of the babyfaced riders wore long green windcheaters with a lashing of false fur around the collar. Those on foot, with creamy complexions and flouncy hairstyles, breezed along in hush puppies with a contrived look of importance that befitted a medieval doctor on an emergency visit. The Mods proved more popular with girls than the greasy Rockers, who removed the baffles from bike exhausts and roared around the city centre roundabout, hoping to impress the large gathering of females parked in shop doorways awaiting their dates.

However, a long tiring trek to Skegness with the gang put me off being a biker for good. Ill prepared, without enough money or proper clothing, we spent an exhausting weekend roaming from café to café hounded by police wishing to prevent a confrontation between us and the gangs of lads on scooters. Next morning, after spending a freezing night in a beach hut, I decided to sell the bike. So I removed my L-plates and drove the ninety miles home down the M1 at eighty miles an hour and arrived with a sizzling engine belching out smoke in all directions. Of course then I could get only a fraction of the original price, leaving myself with a huge debt to pay off.

At work, a choice was presented to me. I could either continue to enjoy the excellent remuneration that piecework provided, or take a substantial drop in wages and attend college at the factory's expense. I accepted the opportunity to obtain a skill and endeavoured to understand a world of measuring instruments and engineering principles. Now I had almost nothing with which to pay off the bike debt or attend the Locarno dancehall, which hosted the many bands that had mushroomed all over the country. Waves of pop hysteria washed over the city and mothers were besieged as youngsters turned front rooms into dens of practice. A friend's parents, astounded by their son's prowess as a musician, did not mind us pounding out the 'sixties sounds in their home. He became addicted to the blues, and had to listen to a record only a couple of times before he could belt out the fuzzy numbers of Hendrix, Black Sabbath, Eric Clapton, or John Mayall and the Blues Breakers. In the knowledge that music was an inherent quality in our family, I accompanied my friend on a cheap electric guitar, trying to emulate the lilting sounds of Hank Marvin and the Shadows.

Some mornings before departing for the factory, Aunt Minnie would ask me to attend to messages on the way home. These were simple errands such as collecting newspapers from the corner shop. To her dismay I arrived home most evenings empty-handed, always presenting the same excuse: 'I never thought.' Fed up with my forgetfulness she eventually questioned the wisdom of my taking the tablets. In her opinion they were preventing me from thinking.

Now nearly eighteen, my lack of progress at work and college really distressed me. Unable to cope with the lectures I became a butt for taunts and cruel jokes. Lads my own age were forging ahead, and I had only one sympathetic friend. Despite his help, I failed my exams, and my standing at work sank lower and lower to a point where I despaired as to what to do with my life. My humiliation was yet to be completed. As a last chance, I was allowed to join an intake of apprentices three years my junior. We spent three months in a newly established training centre built within the factory. The harsh facts now emerged as stark as a winter's morning. I had made a terrible mistake in attempting to become an engineer. At the end of the training programme, I failed yet another exam, which resulted in my being taken off the course and demoted to a welding job under the supervision of a melancholy Geordie. Life had dealt my new tutor some bitter disappointments and while he warned me harshly that this was my last chance, I felt he sympathized.

The occupant which had lain quietly within me during these woolly months rose up again. It pierced my eyes with a fierce anger and prickled my skin with burning heat. That night I put the tin of Mysoline tablets into my pocket and walked to Spencer Park. A fast train rattled by, leaving behind it a welcome void of silence. I flung the tablets with all my might and watched them scatter amidst the web of rusty iron carcasses on the railway line. Wandering home, a calm determination convinced me that now I would re-structure my life. I did not tell Aunt Minnie what I had done. Life at home was changing: the blanket of warmth which had covered me was slipping; friction and sometimes cross words crept in, leaving an atmosphere that made me feel an encumbrance.

A year later I still felt frustrated at not having made much progress. I yearned for a girlfriend, but did not have the confidence. My boxing career was over, my wish to be a skilled man a cruel illusion. This was not what I had planned, it was time to move on: to be alone and independ-ent, and to carve out by whichever way possible a life of material and emotional satisfaction. Two days later I bid my surprised aunt goodbye and headed off to live in the first of many digs.

A quiet room at the top of a house was ideal for concentrating my mind. However, my privacy was short-lived. One evening, returning home late, I discovered two Irish students kneeling in prayer at the foot of the bed opposite mine. Completely oblivious to my presence, they continued mumbling and shuffling their rosary beads. The situation struck me as hilarious. Without thinking, I inter-rupted the Hail Marys and asked them if they had lost something. Deeply offended, they ran downstairs and complained to the landlady. An apology saved me from being tipped out onto the street and from there on I saved my sense of humour for the more appreciative.

Body-building, which I started in order to gain weight, appealed to me and I joined the factory club, run by Jimmy White, a square-jawed Dubliner. Jim, a power-house of a man and an excellent instructor, took a keen interest in my progress. Under his guidance I switched from body-building to weight-lifting. I took to lifting naturally and the energy I exerted put an end to the troublesome stomach cramps. After winning my first contest I was awarded a Junior Certificate of Merit. A few months later, to my astonishment, Jim entered me for the County Championship. Protesting that I was not good enough made no difference and the following Saturday I was whisked off to Birmingham Athletic Institute.

After warming up I walked out of the gymnasium and stood in a toilet cubicle. Here was my chance to become champion and instil pride and belief in myself. In an eye-blinding moment of emotion I thought of my father, and wished he could be there. An aggressive confidence filled me with warmth as I watched Jim power his way to a title. When my turn came I attacked the weights savagely and though I could hear Jim roaring encouragement I did not need it. All my lifts were given three white lights and I became the new county champion. The happiness I experienced then was surpassed only when I read the glowing reports in the next day's *Coventry Evening Telegraph*. Some weeks later I was selected to be in the Coventry team competing against the Bristol champions. Again the words in the local paper filled me with pride:

'Record broken in double over Bristol.'

Winning the competition was wonderful but equally exhilarating was the publicity. There in the middle of the sports page was a full-blown picture of myself completing a lift, with a caption underneath – CONCENTRATION AND DE-TERMINATION ILLUSTRATED ON THE FACE OF JOHN HUGHES DURING THE JUNIOR SQUAT LIFT.

Something else besides pride came out of victory. I now realized that the energy burning within was not, as I had sometimes feared, a destructive force but an invisible companion I could call upon when help was needed.

In 1967, after breaking two county records, I was forced to retire from weight-lifting because of a serious back injury.

I knew that to be mobile was an advantage in the pursuit of girls so, having denied my epilepsy, I passed my driving test and bought a battered mini van. City-centre pubs and the newly built Lanchester Polytechnic College proved the ideal hunting-ground for lads on the prowl. Compared with today's ring of caution generated by increased sexual violence, girls expected approaches from boys in herring-bone suits, swaggering to The Kinks' sleepy music.

Local venues were packed out for The Who's violent performances, which normally ended with the smashing of expensive equipment on stage. A lot of their fans saw this as an expression of freedom, but to me it was wanton destruction designed to whip up feelings in an era which threatened to see liberty and love pushed beyond the tolerance of society.

Gradually I moved away from the town scene, prompted by a menace that was becoming a disturbing fashion. In dark corners of pubs and recessed shop doorways shady characters passed purple hearts, drugs which changed an-gelic faces into elongated distortions like the reflected images in a hall of mirrors. Now my only visits to town were for a different purpose. Running the van was proving impossible, despite cheap repairs from my new landlord, and I began to buy and sell anything I could.

Finally, a two-week wild caravan holiday in Devon with the many friends I had amassed fully initiated me into the free love of the 'sixties. The freedom of those days came through music and fashion, and a sense of unity among teenagers, not the rebellious uprising of the nation's youth.

Lack of privacy was a condition I could not abide and, whilst sorry to say goodbye to the best landlord I had ever met, I moved into my own flat.

Exiled Irishmen are a sentimental lot affected by songs and panning memories of their green and distant land. I was approaching twenty-one and the legal fight against William for my share of the farms, so I could not allow nostalgia to get in the way. Yet when I heard the gravelly voices of the Dubliners singing 'Black Velvet Band' in the club next door, I slipped back to our farmyard and relived precious moments, watching father tap his foot in time to the tune he played best. To prevent feelings of loneliness and isolation unsettling my life, I likened families to birds in a nest, there to be pushed out and left to fend for themselves.

A few months later, after a broken romance, I left the grey depressing factory and embarked on a new career in sales. The year I spent on the road as a travelling salesman selling clothes and household items gave me an insight into the lives of poorer people. A smoky mining village on the outskirts of the city was typical of the drab areas preyed upon by credit companies selling their overpriced goods. Most of the unfortunate customers could not afford the payments collected by representatives driving like maniacs around the streets in order to beat one another to a call. It was well known that some unscrupulous employees pocketed customers' money without signing their payment card. Such was the turn-around in staff who were put off by poverty and dirty-faced children, their fraudulent methods went undetected. While suffering financial hardship myself, I was never tempted to cheat the very people I could identify with. Once I satisfied myself that a case was genuine, I did not pressurize those women who missed payments in order to provide food for their hungry families.

This, however, was not the case with a brazen redhead whose debt of three hundred and seventy-nine pounds had been reduced by only one payment of one and sixpence in eighteen months. I was determined to see the account cleared and embarked on a plan, confident that she could be persuaded to pay up. Charlie Wilson, who stood over six feet and weighed eighteen stone, had just arrived from Derry where during a night of rioting his house and car had been burnt out. When the final attempt to extract money from my fast-talking customer failed, I warned her that next week I would bring a bailiff from Belfast with me who would be taking over the round. Charlie loved my idea and the fat on his huge midriff wobbled with laughter as I drew the van up near the house concerned. I walked briskly up the garden path and rattled the knocker. Opening the door quickly, the woman stood poker-faced and snapped, 'Yes, what do you want?'

Charlie edged forward and I said solemnly, 'Missus, this is the bailiff from Belfast.'

Without altering her expression she roared, 'Well, I'm the belly dancer from Dublin, now fuck off,' and slammed the door.

The effect was mortifying for a few seconds until the funny side struck us and together we laughed on her doorstep till our sides ached. Unable to work, we retired to a working man's club and giggled throughout the afternoon without talking to one another. Eventually my face hurt so much that I had to bid Charlie goodbye with a wave of my hand. I never saw him again. Handing back my keys and stock the next afternoon, I learned he had resigned that morning.

At twenty-four, my legal battle with William ended. My tenacious solicitor, fed up with derisory offers and delaying tactics, secured a hearing in the Chancery Division of the Belfast High Court. An eleventh-hour compromise suggested by my brother was accepted; this included my agreement to take one thousand pounds as a deposit with a balance of eight hundred pounds to be paid over the course of twelve months. The years of scrimping and living in dismal flats came to an end and I used my modest inheritance and savings to purchase a place of my own.

Optimism and determination are qualities I am grateful to possess. Being a successful salesman, I was much in demand around the city's furniture shops, yet while enjoying good earnings my desire to progress towards total independence grew stronger. I revelled in the field of sales and, with the inhibiting effect of Mysoline all but gone, learning came quickly. Against the advice of friends, I sold my home, furniture and car and started my own business in 1973 as a bedding specialist. The shop, a former butcher's premises, was very cold, damp and small. Other than selling, I had no knowledge of business matters, but now I had even greater reason to succeed as I had met the person I wanted to marry.

My latter years in retail were shared with a passion for

redeveloping property, and after restoring and leasing out an old Victorian building in 1987 I finally realized the security I had craved as a boy.

I left Ireland to be free of oppression and restriction but ironically I had to return there to be published. As I write these last words in the bright light of my drawing-room, I acknowledge my fortune. I did not know love as a child. I do now, and it is wonderful.